Praise for *Raising Kids* . . . . . .

"*Raising Kids Who Can* elucidates several profoundly important childrearing goals. The central concept of the book, which proposes family meetings as a technique of intimacy and honesty, will help parents raise children who have the skill and the will to distinguish themselves as human beings in a changing society."
—**Letty Cottin Pogrebin, founding member of *Ms.* magazine and author of *Among Friends* and *Family Politics***

"*Raising Kids Who Can* is a welcome addition to the parent education library. Bettner and Lew have created a fresh, insightful synthesis of strategies for becoming a more functional, responsible, and capable family."
—**Don Dinkmeyer, Jr., coauthor of *Preparing Responsible and Effective Parents* (PREP) and *Systematic Training for Effective Teachers***

"Thumbs up to a great book! What good news and hope it brings to today's bewildered parents. The dream of every Mom and Dad is to have their kids turn out capable, responsible, respectful, and courageous. These concrete, practical, time-tested strategies will help make this dream come true."
—**Linda Albert, syndicated columnist and author of the Coping with Kids series**

"*Raising Kids Who Can* offers a useful, sensible, caring, respectful approach that all families can benefit from. My family held its first meeting last night and we plan on continuing. This book gave me the impetus and inspiration to get it going."
—Ellen Bass, coauthor of *The Courage to Heal*

"*Raising Kids Who Can* is solidly informative, enormously readable, and slim enough for busy people to squeeze into their lives."
—Linda Jessup, radio talk show host and director of the Parent Encouragement Program

"This book, while providing the nuts and bolts of family meetings, is really much more. Bettner and Lew have produced one of those rare finds in the self-help literature that translates into immediate and positive change for families."
—Frank Main, Professor of Counseling, University of South Dakota, and author of *Perfect Parenting and Other Myths*

"Learn the how-tos of cooperative living from this all-encompassing family meeting manual."
—Evonne Weinhaus and Karen Friedman, authors of *Stop Struggling with Your Child* and *Stop Struggling with Your Teen*

"*Raising Kids Who Can* is a comprehensive, clear and concise new 'must' for parents, counselors, therapists and schools."
—Bobbi Moritz, Director, Family Education Center of the South Shore, Centreville, Massachusetts

RAISING KIDS WHO CAN

RAISING KIDS WHO CAN

Using Family Meetings

to Nurture Responsible,

Cooperative, Caring,

and Happy Children

Betty Lou Bettner, Ph.D., and Amy Lew, Ph.D.

Illustrations by
John Mahoney

HarperPerennial
A Division of HarperCollins*Publishers*

HarperCollins books may be purchased for educational, business, or sales promotional use. For information, please call or write: Special Markets Department, HarperCollins Publishers, Inc., 10 East 53rd Street, New York, NY 10022. Telephone: (212) 207-7528; Fax: (212) 207-7222.

First HarperPerennial edition published 1992.

Designed by Jessica Shatan

Library of Congress Cataloging-in-Publication Data

Bettner, Betty Lou.
Raising kids who can: using family meetings to nurture responsible, cooperative, caring, and happy children / Betty Lou Bettner and Amy Lew: illustrations by John Mahoney — 1st HarperPerennial ed.
    p.   cm.
Includes bibliographical references.
ISBN 0-06-096932-6 (pbk.)
1. Communication in the family—United States.
2. Child rearing—United States. I. Lew, Amy.
II. Title. III. Title: Family meetings.
HQ518.B48   1992
649′.1—dc20   91-58459

---

92 93 94 95 96 CC/CW 10 9 8 7 6 5 4 3 2 1

To families everywhere,
on behalf of Rudolf Dreikurs, who taught:

"Democracy must start at home . . . each one participating in its establishment, experimenting and exploring all avenues until those best suited for the common good are found. Then we have a natural order based on freedom for all and on a sense of responsibility that characterizes free [humans] everywhere."

—*Social Equality: The Challenge of Today*

Contents

Acknowledgments

Perhaps the most difficult part of writing a book is trying to accurately convey our gratitude to the many people who have encouraged, nurtured, and helped us along the way.

We wish to thank our husbands, Frank and Walt, who willingly read through the many drafts of the manuscript, listened to our endless suggestions for a title, put up with our long absences, watched the kids, and often made us lunch.

Our conviction about the value of family meetings comes from our personal experience with our own families. We are grateful to our children and many clients and study-group participants for sharing with us a wealth of experience and stories.

We especially thank our own children: Sarah and Kate; Mark, Michelle, Matthew, and Todd; and those we borrowed: Robbie, Alice, Bill, Kenny, Donnie, Dawn, Richie, Pete, Debbie, Billy, Charles, Ben, Diane, Michael, Joe, Lydia, Melissa, Andrei, Lisa, Kas, and Fran for providing us with the evidence that family meetings work. We would like to express our appreciation to our parents and extended families for giving us the foundation from which to grow.

We have been fortunate to have had the encouragement and guidance of many Adlerian teachers and friends. In particular we wish to acknowledge Drs. Manford Sonstegard and Raymond Lowe for introducing us to Adlerian counseling. We have also learned much from our colleagues at the North American Society of Adlerian Psychology and the International Committee of Adlerian Summer Schools and Institutes.

Thanks also go to those who offered editorial assistance: Linda Albert, Bobbi Moritz, Emily Thorn, Linda Jessup, Howard Garrell, Jean Lonberg, and to our marketing and design consultants for the first edition, Greenebaum & Greenebaum.

Special thanks to Chris Polischuk for her generous artistic contribution to the Agenda for Families of Young Children, and Mary Susan Convery for her administrative assistance.

We are, of course, indebted to Alfred Adler and Rudolf Dreikurs for developing the theory and techniques that provide the inspiration for all of our work.

Preface for the New Edition

We wrote the preface for the 1990 edition of *Raising Kids Who Can* confident about the usefulness of family meetings and hopeful that we would be able to reach a wide and varied audience. The initial response to the book has confirmed our confidence.

In the spring of 1990 we were invited to the Soviet Union to teach psychologists, psychiatrists, and educators about Adlerian psychology and parenting techniques. The response was overwhelmingly enthusiastic. The formerly Soviet republics are well aware that raising children for a democratic system requires qualities and abilities far different from those necessary for survival in an autocratic society. Abilities such as taking initiative, assuming responsibility, evaluating information, making decisions for themselves, and communicating effectively are especially important for people who will be asked to vote and participate in the post-perestroika republics. An Estonian translation of the book has been completed and will be published this year.

Other countries have also expressed interest in distributing *Raising Kids Who Can*. A German edition was released early in 1992 and the English version has been warmly received in Australia, Ireland, Greece, and Israel. In the United States, Canada, and Puerto Rico numerous parent-education groups have used the book as a basis for a five-week course.

We have also been contacted by many professionals who have found the book useful in various settings. Therapists working with drug and alcohol abusers in treatment centers are using the family meeting to open communication, identify and build on strengths, and provide a model for constructive conflict resolution. Clients are then encouraged to initiate meetings upon returning to their homes in order to break old patterns and establish new forms of interaction. Initial findings point to a marked decrease in recidivism among those clients who have initiated family meetings.

Adults raised in troubled families are also finding our book extremely useful. Having experienced destructive parenting themselves, they are concerned about their own ability to parent constructively. Family meetings provide them with an open, encouraging structure for developing healthy families.

Family meetings are also being successfully used in institutions for children. Children who have experienced group meetings begin to talk about their concerns and feelings instead of acting out.

The practical applications of family meetings abound. We would appreciate hearing from you about your experiences.

Preface

As marriage and family therapists who are actively involved in parent and teacher education, we hear a lot of concern about the future of the family. People worry about the high incidence of teenage drug and alcohol abuse, teen gangs and vandalism, and the general alienation of our youth. They also worry about the growing number of divorces and unwed mothers and the "me first" attitude of many of our young adults.

Many professionals tell parents that they should lay down the law, make stricter rules, and demand obedience; but, as any parent of teenagers knows, it's a lot easier to *make* the rules than to *enforce* them. The parents that we meet are often discouraged by this advice. They try to "make" their kids behave and instead find that there is either a defiant escalation of misbehavior or a withdrawal and hiding of what the children are doing. Whatever positive relationship there may have been is eroded by the parents' becoming distrustful "law" enforcers.

Educators and counselors try desperately to find solutions. Many high schools, colleges, and religious groups give courses in family living. Although we see the value in any attempt at prevention, we believe these interventions should begin much sooner. Premarital counseling in nursery school?—well, maybe. That is the time when children should begin to learn how to cooperate, take responsibility, solve problems, and communicate openly. By the time kids are young adults or ready to get married they have already learned bad habits.

We spend the first years encouraging our children to be competitive by making comparisons with their siblings and peers, telling them they are too small, too young, or too incompetent; and then we are surprised that they are not prepared to become contributing, independent, well-functioning adults. We wonder why couples have trouble cooperating in a marriage, yet few people have had any previous training in cooperation.

Rudolf Dreikurs, a prominent Adlerian psychiatrist, devoted much of his life to developing principles that would help parents, teachers, and other adults who work with children. Basing his work on Alfred Adler's theory of individual psychology, Dreikurs developed a common-sense, practical approach for raising courageous children who will have the skills to meet life's challenges constructively, and who can avoid the major pitfalls and dangers that confront children in today's society. We will be expanding on one of these important skills—*the family meeting*.

In this book we will show you how you can use the family meeting to reduce the probability of raising a high-risk, dependent adolescent and increase the probability of raising an independent and capable adult. In addition you will learn the essential perceptions and skills that all children need to become successful adults and how the development of these perceptions and skills is encouraged in the family meeting.

Betty Lou Bettner
Media, Pennsylvania

Amy Lew
Newton Centre, Massachusetts

RAISING KIDS WHO CAN

Introduction

Parenting with a Purpose

As parents we are all familiar with the discussions about quality time versus quantity time. Which is better? How much of either is enough? When should you do which? Both are important to different degrees as our children grow and develop. Infants and toddlers need lots of caretaking, and, therefore, require more "quantity time." Exhausted by 7 P.M., we need to remind ourselves that the "quality time" *will* come someday! As our children develop, the quantity of our time with them decreases and the quality of our interactions increases. If all goes according to plan, by the time they become adults the quantity of time with them will diminish to occasional visits and the quality of our time with them will increase to that of friends.

"Qualities" Time

In order for this to happen, however, we have to invest some effort in what could be called "qualities" time. This is the time we spend fostering the qualities we would like to see in our children, qualities such as honesty, responsibility, courage, respect, confidence, productivity, self-esteem, self-discipline, and cooperativeness. These are qualities that are valued by most parents, needed by society, and necessary for becoming an independent, contributing adult.

H. Stephen Glenn, former director of the National Drug Abuse Center for Training and Resource Development, states that when these qualities are missing our young people run the risk of getting into trouble. His extensive research into such diverse issues as drug and alcohol abuse, teenage pregnancy, delinquency, and underachievement point to a common personality profile—that of a chronically dependent person. Dependent people do not see themselves as contributing members of society. They see what they deserve, what others should do for them, and why they should be excused from chores, school, work, and other requirements of social living. They are some of the casualties of the "Me Generation." These people don't see what they have to offer to others, or why they should owe anything to anybody. Those who are chronically dependent lack both the desire and the skills needed for becoming fully functioning adults.

Although we are born dependent on others for survival, we all have the desire to grow and become independent. The apparent contradiction between needing others, being needed by others, and needing to be self-sufficient results in what Alfred Adler, one of the founders of modern psychology, described as three basic desires common to all people.

What Kids Need to Succeed

The "Three Cs"

1. Everyone wants to belong, to feel *connected*. Human babies are dependent upon others to survive. They must quickly develop ways to fit into their families in order to get the care they need. The strategies they develop in order to connect with this first group (their family) will set the stage for connecting with others throughout their lives. Children who develop positive connections with their families feel secure. This necessary sense of security enables them to reach out and identify with others in a positive way.

2. Everyone wants to feel *capable* and competent. In order to develop a sense of security, self-respect, and self-esteem, people must believe that they can take care of themselves and handle what life brings. Children who grow up in families where they are allowed to test their competencies in a safe atmosphere, without fear of humiliation, are able to believe in themselves and in their ability to solve problems.

3. Everyone wants to feel significant, to *count*. People want to feel that they make a difference, that their existence matters. If children feel that their contributions to their families are appreciated and necessary, they will feel confident and willing to contribute elsewhere.

These desires, which we call the "Three Cs" (to be connected, to feel capable, and to count) may be fulfilled through constructive means or through socially useless methods. People may feel connected because they belong to the community *or* to a gang. People may feel capable of taking on responsibility *or* may make a career out of avoiding doing what is expected of them. People may feel that they count when they contribute *or* they may find their significance through misbehavior or self-elevation. Teen gangs and cults provide all three Cs through negative means.

Essential Skills and Abilities

In order for the Three Cs to be fulfilled constructively a person must also develop the following four important sets of skills:

1. The ability to *communicate*—which includes being able to express oneself clearly and being able to listen to others. These interpersonal skills are necessary for making friends, joining groups, finding success in careers, and developing intimacy. Weaknesses in this area show up as dishonesty with others, lack of empathy, inability to share feelings, and difficulty in giving and receiving love or help.

2. The ability to use good *judgment*—which requires openness to new information, the ability to see alternatives, the courage to make decisions, and the willingness to evaluate those choices. Without these skills people find themselves in a continual series of crises. They may overindulge in any number of areas: spending, alcohol, drugs, leisure, sex, and so on, because they are unable to recognize, understand, or apply effective solutions to their problems.

3. The ability to assume *responsibility*—which requires recognizing limits, identifying what needs to be done, and being willing to meet the needs of the situation. People without these skills may refuse to accept the consequences of their behavior. They tend to scapegoat others, blame the system, or see themselves as victims.

4. The ability to be *self-disciplined*—which requires self-evaluation, self-understanding, recognition of one's own feelings, goals, and attitudes; and the willingness to accept responsibility for personal actions. Weaknesses in this area result in people who look to others to decide if they are right or wrong. They compare themselves to others and worry about "how" they are doing rather than "what" they are doing. They seem unable to cope with pressure or stress. They have low self-esteem, are unable to be honest with themselves, and often have difficulty with deferring gratification.

We would like to add to this list of skills two qualities that are necessary for success in life. The first, *courage*, enables us to face failure, to pick ourselves up when we fall down, to take risks and try new things. The second, the *ability to cooperate*, allows us to join in and become members of a team.

The development of the above skills and qualities, which are so crucial to a person's life, cannot be left to chance. They *must* be cultivated and nurtured. Although nothing we do can guarantee that our children will turn out exactly the way we want them to, we can increase the likelihood of producing capable, well-adjusted young people if we put thought and effort into our parenting techniques.

The first thing we need to do is evaluate our present techniques to see if they promote the development of the qualities that we have seen are so critical. We can accomplish this evaluation by answering the following questions about our current parenting techniques:

1. Are they stopping misbehavior?
2. Are they developing the qualities I value in my child?
3. What kind of opinion does my child seem to be forming of him/herself and others?
4. Does my child act as a contributing member of society, or does he/she act as if the world is there to serve him/her?

If any of the answers to these questions are unsatisfactory, we must come up with a new plan.

Making It Happen

We need two kinds of parenting techniques:

1. Direct techniques, which allow us to check out our children's perceptions and make sure that we are providing the opportunity for them to learn and practice important skills for life.

2. Indirect techniques, which we use daily in all of our interactions with each other and which set the tone for family living.

At this point many parents begin to panic. "Where will we find the time? With all the things we have to do each day we're lucky if we can get our kids to all their scheduled activities, eat a meal together, and ask about their day." Parents are amazed to find out that by setting aside thirty to sixty minutes each week for a family meeting they can have a powerful influence on the development of all of these vital qualities.

The Adlerian family meeting is a direct approach, which ensures that children get a chance to learn firsthand, through experience and observation, all of the essential skills. Through scheduled, structured weekly meetings family members reinforce their *connection*. Compliments, appreciations, problem solving, and decision-making components of the family meeting point out strengths and help all members see that they are *capable*. Children feel that they *count* when they see that what they do makes a difference and that they are capable of making necessary contributions. Since family meeting participants experience themselves as competent, important members of the family group, they develop courage and learn to be considerate of others.

In order for the family meeting to be successful, parents should learn, use, and teach two types of indirect techniques as well. These indirect techniques are *encouragement* and *logical discipline*. Encouragement develops self-esteem, self-reliance, courage, and a sense of competence. The use of logical discipline demonstrates the importance of social order, teaches cause and effect, and fosters self-evaluation, good judgment, and responsibility. These techniques are more fully described in Parts II and III.

The combination of these important indirect techniques with the direct approach of the family meeting is a uniquely powerful vehicle for creating an atmosphere where children can develop all of the skills and qualities necessary to become independent, productive citizens. Our goal is to raise children who *can* say no to drugs, who *will* make wise decisions about alcohol and sexual activity, and who *want* to connect, to be capable, and feel that they count by making a contribution to society.

PART I

The Family Meeting

Chapter 1

Getting Started

Family meetings mean something different to each member of the family.

With today's hectic schedules most plans and decisions are made on the run. Parents usually make all of the arrangements, plan the activities, hand out the chores, and get annoyed or angry when the kids don't appreciate all that is done for them. The kids, on the other hand, are likely to feel bossed around and discounted since they've been left out of the planning and decision making.

John and Mary were distressed by their kids' refusal to share and play with the children of invited guests. They couldn't understand why their children weren't more friendly and welcoming. After a long lecture about appropriate behavior, they finally got around to asking the kids for an explanation. Mom and Dad were taken aback by their children's simple reply, "We don't like those kids and we didn't invite them." John and Mary realized that it wasn't the children who had forgotten their manners; it was the parents. Mom and Dad could see that they wouldn't have been too happy if their kids had invited friends' parents over without asking and then expected Mom and Dad to do the entertaining.

When families take the time to sit down together to decide what needs to be done and how to do it, everyone may be surprised at the result. Parents who have experienced fighting with their kids over taking out the garbage may discover that when the children have input into which chores they will do they are more likely to take on responsibility and remember to follow through. Successful meetings help family members learn to share responsibility and solve problems together.

One way to get started is to have one parent introduce the idea by saying, "I read about a neat idea that many families use for organizing themselves, making plans, and working out problems. I would like to try this approach in our family, maybe for a month, and see if it works for us. Would you be willing to give it a try?" This may not always work, however; parents will probably have a sense of whether being straightforward or indirect will be more effective in their situation.

Some parents, excited about the idea of family meetings, expect that their kids will also see the value in it. Even if the parents say that the meeting is a great way for family members to talk to each other, have a say in the way things are handled, and increase cooperation, children may be suspicious when the meeting is first brought up. The kids may think that the parents have just come up with a new method to get them to do what the parents want. Kids may not be so far off, since adults often ask for "cooperation" when they actually mean "Do as I say!"

One good way to circumvent this problem is to start off slowly. Instead of introducing the family meeting all at once, parents can introduce the idea of family problem solving and decision making by simply asking everyone to get together for a specific purpose, such as planning a family activity. When fun is involved, most people are intrigued and are usually willing to take a chance.

With older kids parents might invite them to discuss borrowing the car, allowances, or some other privilege. The main point is that the topics should be of interest to the kids.

Everyone Counts

In order to show that each person's opinion is valued, make sure that everyone knows of the plans to meet. Come up with a time when everyone is available even if some won't commit to coming. If everyone is available, someone who was reluctant at first will at least have an opportunity to change that decision. If everyone is invited and no one is forced, each person can feel wanted and respected. *Each person counts.*

"Why don't we all give some thought to what we might do this weekend and get together tomorrow evening and make some plans."

"Dad, I won't be here tomorrow. I have hockey practice."

"Okay, when would be a good time for all of us?"

Another way to show respect is by sharing information that the kids will need in order to come up with feasible suggestions. If there are any special limitations on the plans, such as time, money, or distance, state them before the meeting.

> "I sure hope we get lots of suggestions from everyone, but while you're thinking, try to come up with ideas that don't cost more than twenty-five dollars because that's all Mom and I can come up with."

If this information isn't given before the decision making begins, children may feel that parents are arbitrarily rejecting their ideas. Fighting and distrust may follow. If the limits are stated first, everyone is put in the same boat with equal responsibility and opportunity to make informed suggestions and decisions. This is important training for citizens in a democracy.

The themes of respect and "freedom within limits" are continued throughout the structure of the meeting. Everyone is encouraged to participate. Everyone is listened to. All ideas are considered.

> "We're all here and we have an hour before bedtime, so why don't we begin by doing a little brainstorming?" (For younger children an explanation of brainstorming may be required; e.g., "That's when everyone gives ideas, and you can give as many as you like. We can make a list of all the suggestions. They can be funny or serious or anywhere in between, since sometimes one person's silly idea helps others to think of another idea.") "Remember, this is just a time for coming up with lots of ideas. We will talk about them and give our opinions later."

Try to give everyone a chance to speak so that all ideas are heard.

"How about if we put the timer on for five minutes and see how many ideas we can think of in that time."

Family Connection

Write all the ideas down on paper that's large enough to hang up for everyone to see. This simple idea makes it clear that it's a family project. The child's *connection* to the family is underscored. The next step is to evaluate each of the suggestions in light of the agreed-upon limitations. Keep the discussion open so that each member can say what she or he would like to do and why.

"Wow, look at this list. We did a great job. I think four heads are better than one. I bet there are lots of things on this list that we would all enjoy doing. How shall we decide?"

"We could look the list over to see if we will have to eliminate anything because it would cost more than the twenty-five dollars we have to spend or it would take longer than the Saturday we have available."

"I guess the trip to Disneyworld is out, but maybe we could plan on doing that when we talk about a vacation for next year."

"We could each take a different-color crayon and put a star next to any of the ideas that we might like to do (even if we didn't suggest them and even if they are not our favorites). Let's just see how many of these ideas are ones we all like."

"Why don't we all give three of our favorites and see if anything shows up on everyone's list?"

"There's one suggestion that came up as first or second choice from all of us—going to the movies. Should we go to the matinee or the evening show? If we go to the bargain show, we could probably have enough money to stop for something to eat afterward. What do each of you think about that?"

If someone is not agreeing and others are ganging up, getting angry, or trying to apply some sort of pressure, the parent can reestablish a respectful atmosphere by adding a statement of support.

"Ron, if Mike doesn't want to go to the movies I wouldn't want him to give in and not have a good time. The purpose of this meeting was to find something that would be fun for all of us. I think we should respect Mike's decision about what is and isn't fun for him. Perhaps you could bring up the idea of the movie again next week. It's important for us as a family to plan a day that will be fun for all of us."

Each Person Is Capable

Now it is time to discuss what needs to be done to put the plan into action and what responsibility each family member will assume.

"What time should we leave? Who will find out what time the show starts? Does anyone know how much money we'll need? Do we want to have a snack before we leave or do we want to get something there?" (If another activity had been selected, the discussion might include other requirements, such as food, equipment, or transportation.)

Allowing each member of the group to take some responsibility for carrying out the plan gives each person a chance to feel important through contribution. A list of responsibilities could be developed so that each member will have a way to take part. (A small child can get the newspaper that lists the movie or do some other task that may be required.) In this way even the youngest members of the family can experience themselves as capable and necessary members of the family group.

Sometimes a family can't settle on one idea. If this happens, the parent(s) can suggest another time when everyone can meet and make more suggestions or reconsider those already mentioned. Keep a friendly tone of voice.

"Well, it looks like we have to stop for now because it's bedtime. Why don't we all give this some more thought and set a time later this week when we could talk again."

At this point there may be one person who has been turning ideas down and now grudgingly agrees to go along with one of the ideas. When the parent realizes that the child is giving in, some encouraging remark can be given.

"Mike, we don't want you to agree to do something that will not feel enjoyable to you. We'll meet again and come to a decision. It's not essential that we decide right now. We'll get another chance."

Future Meetings

In order to introduce the idea of an expanded meeting parents might ask the kids for their input and feedback about how the planning session went.

Do you think this method for deciding what we would do worked well? What would you change about how we did it? What made it fun? Was there anything you didn't like? What other topics do you think we could discuss at a meeting like this?

Families may need several planning sessions before they develop the trust and skills necessary to add further agenda items.

As you can see, even a simple discussion to plan an enjoyable activity can provide a valuable opportunity to strengthen the "Three Cs" and develop skills and abilities. Each person counts, is capable, and is connected to the family. Children and adults learn to listen and share, take responsibility, treat each other respectfully, and participate in decision making.

The Family Goal

As families see the advantages of establishing a weekly family meeting, they are usually anxious to develop it more fully. In Part I we talked about fostering the qualities we would like to see our children develop. Now we have the opportunity to think about, and foster, the qualities we would like to see in our families. These qualities may vary from family to family. They are the specific characteristics that each family aspires to, or what we call the "family goal."

In order to make sure that the meeting is the family's meeting and not just the parents' meeting it is important to include the whole family in defining the "family goal." If children feel that only the parents' desires are taken into account, they are less likely to feel invested in achieving these goals.

Parents can introduce the idea of the "family goal" in several ways:

When children are very little the parents decide how the family should be. Now that you are older we would like to hear what you think and decide together what kind of family we're going to have.

What would our family look like if it was the way you wanted it to be?

We know that you're a teenager now and may be thinking about leaving this family or that it's not worth trying to make things better, but we would like to make the best of the time we have left together. Can you think of what this new and improved family might look like?

When you start your own family, how would you like it to be?

In order to avoid put-downs, insults, arguments, and defensiveness, people are asked to focus on what they would like to see in their family, not what they don't like about it.

(don't like)	"I hate the way Tommy is always whining."
(would like)	"I would like people to speak nicely to each other."
(don't like)	"I wish people would stop bugging me."
(would like)	"I'd like people to respect my privacy."
(don't like)	"I can't stand it when Susie is so snobby and won't let anybody near her room."
(would like)	"I'd like to spend more time with Susie."

Since we want all members of the family to feel that their ideas count and that they are capable of making a contribution, we ask each person to write down (or in the case of younger children, dictate) what kind of family he or she would like. It is important that everyone has the opportunity to come up with his or her own ideas before sharing with the others. In this way everyone gives the subject some real thought and no one is prematurely influenced by someone else's ideas. It is important to make sure that everyone knows that nobody's ideas will be put down or judged.

An added benefit for the parents is that they get a unique

opportunity to hear what is of real value to their children. Some parents may be surprised by what they hear.

A family had sought counseling for a teenage son's rebellious behavior (staying out all night, failing several subjects in school). When each one was asked to answer "how I would like my family to be," the son wrote "I'd like us to eat dinner together more often; I'd like more family vacations; I'd like it if people didn't ask me so many questions." The parents were shocked; they thought that their son couldn't wait to get away from them. While he did want more independence and he wanted them to trust him more, he also wanted more closeness.

When everyone has finished writing, it is time for sharing. Each person takes a turn reading his or her ideas and having the other members of the family respond. Feedback might take the form of "what I agree/disagree with," "what surprises me," "what I don't understand," and so on.

Now it is time to incorporate all of the individual ideas into a statement of the family "goal." First, the family can look over all of the ideas and separate them into two categories: (1) qualities—how we would like the family to be, and (2) actions—what the family needs to do in order to be that way. Examples of qualities are closeness, affection, respect, helpfulness, caring, and cooperation. Examples of actions are having dinner together, kissing goodnight, knocking before entering, helping with homework, listening to someone's concern, and doing chores on time.

Since the "family goal" serves as a guideline or ideal to be strived for, it should be a statement of qualities. The actions a family takes will change with the ages of the children, number in the family, and the needs of the situation. A "family goal" statement might sound like these:

(A family with young children) Our family is a place where everyone feels safe and loved and people help each other. Everyone tries to help others feel important.

(A family with older children) In our family we will respect each other, decisions will be mutually agreed upon, and we will do what we agreed to do.

Once the "family goal" is agreed to, the next step is to return to the "action statements" and ask each family member to think about what he or she could do to reach the "family goal." Each person can then pick one thing to work on for the coming week. It's important to let each person make an unpressured choice. (Suggestions may be perceived as criticism.)

JOHNNY (age five): I'm not going to go into Megan's room without asking.

MEGAN (age fourteen): I'm not going to tease Johnny or call him half-pint.

GEORGE (age eight): I'm going to do my chores without being reminded.

MAX (age seventeen): I'm going to do something special with George once a week.

DAD: I'm going to pay full attention when anyone in my family is talking to me or make a date for when I can.

MOM: I'm going to wait until I'm asked before offering suggestions.

At the next meeting each family member will review his or her own action and evaluate how well it worked. New actions may now be chosen and/or old ones worked on for another week.

The statement of the "family goal" should also be reviewed at this time. If everyone still agrees with it, it is written clearly and put in a prominent place (on the refrigerator, for example,). Any changes should be agreed to by all and reviewed at the next meeting. In the future, when disagreements or conflicts arise, the family can refer to the "family goal" to determine if their solutions and/or actions are bringing them closer or further from the family's stated ideals.

Chapter 2

Creating an Agenda

Not all problems have to be solved immediately.

Once the family has decided to meet on a regular basis it can expand the value of the meeting by developing an agreed-upon agenda, which will meet its particular needs. The agenda may include such items as thank-yous, division of chores, resolving disputes, distributing finances, making plans, getting help with problems, sharing information, and planning family activities.

In the following sections we will be discussing how to set up the structure and create the agenda for the family meeting.

Compliments

No matter what else you may have in your family meeting, it should include a time for encouragement. Most families refer to this agenda item as "Appreciations," "Thank-yous" or "Compliments." This item comes at the beginning of the meeting to set the tone for pleasant communication.

Criticism and complaints are commonplace in most families. Anyone who watches the stereotypical television comedy will count twenty-five to fifty sarcastic put-downs in a half-hour program. Busy and conflicting schedules usually leave little time for anything except hurried instructions and corrections. We need family activities to counteract this faultfinding so that all family members learn the importance of valuing and appreciating each other. Starting the meeting with "Appreciations" guarantees us an opportunity to look deliberately for strengths and to show our children that we notice the positives as well as the negatives.

One way to help the busy family shift gears is to start off with a minute of silence designed to allow participants to formulate their compliments:

I want to thank Dad for picking me up from practice this week.

I want to say how much easier and more enjoyable it was when everyone pitched in and helped clean up for the company last Friday.

I want to compliment Katie on how hard she's been working on her science project.

I want to thank Mark for helping me with my homework.

I want to recognize Melissa's courage in tasting the broc-
coli.

I want to thank Michelle for doing my chore while I was
away.

I want to tell everyone how much I appreciate them for not
yelling at me when I burned the cookies.

I'd like to thank Sarah for her helpful ideas in handling the
bullies at school.

I'd like to tell Matthew how impressed I am with his ability
to stick to his job even though he didn't like his boss.

Although we don't mention it much anymore, I'd like to tell
Todd how proud I am of his hard work and commitment
to his karate.

Each person is given an opportunity (without insisting) to say
a thank-you to anyone in the family for anything that hap-
pened since the last meeting. When parents are eager to say
a thank-you to each person in the family, the children are
quick to follow. In the beginning people may be uncomfort-
able giving and receiving compliments, but everyone likes to
hear good things, and before long this becomes a highlight of
the meeting.

Compliments may be given for family members who were
unable or unwilling to attend the meeting. The meeting
teaches that all are recognized with positive communication.
No one is criticized for not attending, and all are invited to
attend any activity planned even if they were not at the
meeting.

Pointing to a person's strengths is an important part of
building self-esteem and courage. We often find ourselves
complimenting only those who are already successful. Children who consistently misbehave rarely hear people speak
about what they do right. They may become so discouraged

that they decide that the only way others will notice them is if they cause trouble.

Dawn was a discouraged child who was always misbehaving. She was quite used to people pointing out what she did wrong and she felt picked on and angry. When it came time for compliments at the family meeting, everyone had a new experience. Dawn and her family realized that she was not all bad! This change in focus pointed the way for Dawn to find other ways to fit in. It also helped people to regain their warm feelings about Dawn and change their low expectations of her.

The family meeting would be a valuable tool even if the only two things we did were plan activities and appreciate each other. At least then we would know that we could cooperate when we wanted to and that no matter how angry we got at each other during the week, we could always find a few good things to say.

Topics for the Agenda

Each family should adapt the meeting to fulfill its own needs. The meeting is for all family business. Each family will have personal preferences for agenda items. A good first step is to make a list together of all the items for discussion that could be brought up at the meeting, such as:

Household or yard chores
Problems or concerns regarding any family issue or relationship
Care of pets
Announcements
Clothing or personal needs
Family rules

Homework or school projects
Television privileges
Vacations
Family fun
Gifts
Celebrations
Menu suggestions
Overnight or dinner guests
Compliments
Allowances
Special projects

Individual families will probably have items they don't think should be discussed at the meeting. It may be surprising to see how few things cannot be brought up or shared with the group. While final responsibility for making a decision may lie with an individual or the parents, the opinions and concerns of others may provide additional possibilities or valuable insights, and may even influence the final choice.

In order to remind everyone of the agreements and discourage "selective memory," brief notes will be needed. We recommend that families keep the minutes of their meetings in a Family Meeting Notebook. This provides a permanent record of topics, discussions, and decisions. It is important to keep the notebook in a designated spot that is easily accessible to everyone so that all members are free to check the notes for any clarification. Parents don't have to keep reminding or remembering. Those who forget can be asked to check the minutes of the last meeting. Saving the written minutes of each meeting can serve as a journal that provides a nice chronicle of family life.

Some families post an agenda on the refrigerator or bulletin board so that members may add an item whenever they wish. For children who are too young to read, a chart with pictures could be posted so that they could "read" each item. (See appendix.) Another way to develop agenda items is to have appropriate categories that are addressed at each meeting, for example:

- Appreciations and thank-yous
- Minutes from last meeting
- Issues, concerns, and solutions
- Announcements, plans, weekly schedule
- Family needs
- Family jobs
- Family fun activity

When parents are told some news or new information by children, they can remind them: "Be sure to announce that at the family meeting this week." As topics and ideas come up during the week, anyone in the family can suggest that the subject be brought up at the next family meeting. If a topic appears regularly, it can be suggested as a permanent agenda item.

Family Work

If we want our children to feel that they count, we have to let them know that they are needed and valued. If we want them to feel capable we must give them responsibility and allow them to develop their competency through useful contribution to the running of the family.

Each family member should participate in household tasks in order to feel important and capable. Too often, by the time we're ready to "need" kids we've already discouraged them from wanting to contribute.

FOUR-YEAR-OLD: Mommy, can I run the vacuum?

MOMMY: Oh no, dear, you're too little for that job.

TEN-YEAR-OLD: Dad, could I start mowing the lawn this summer?

DAD: No, lawn mowers are too dangerous for kids your age.

Instead of refusing or lecturing the parents could have said:

The hallway hasn't been vacuumed yet and your help would be appreciated. This family needs everyone.

If you were to take on this responsibility, what would you need to know about the lawn-mower operation? What safety precautions would you have to take?

The parents might have been surprised to learn that their children had already carefully studied the situation and had much of the information necessary. When kids ask for more responsibility, it's usually a good indication that they are ready to move on and handle more.

All tasks require cooperation and families that are successful know how to work together and share responsibility. The strongest element in sharing responsibility is mutual respect. When we respect others we don't expect them to handle our responsibilities but we do expect them to handle their responsibilities. Respect means we don't force others nor do we pamper them. We don't push and we don't pull!

Families often report that chores are a constant source of debate. Most people think of a chore as drudgery. Even when there is no anger there is usually a lot of discussion. One way to invite cooperation is to view the jobs necessary for the smooth running of the family as family work instead of chores. Most families who hold weekly meetings put household jobs on the agenda. This item goes more smoothly when:

1. Each member has a say in what jobs need to be done.

2. The group helps to decide *who* will do *what*, and *when*, and *how* they will do it, according to ability. Kids should always be expected to contribute to the family and also be provided training in all house and yard jobs in order to become skillful and self-sufficient and in order to experience a sense of helping and feeling needed.

3. The group discusses and decides what will happen if the jobs aren't done (fail-safes). The consequences of a job undone should apply to everyone. If a parent forgets to do a chore, the child should be allowed to follow the same procedure. Justice under the law begins at home!

4. To avoid confusion, parents can take the family on a tour of each room or task and ask the group, "What do you think needs to be done here?" The instructions can be written down and kept in the back of the Family Meeting Notebook.

The way we speak to our children will also affect whether they feel respected and necessary, or merely bossed around and used. The following are some typical mistaken ways parents try to gain "cooperation" and some alternative suggestions.

Instead of:

"Since you won't choose which job you want, I'll assign one!"

try:

"If you don't want to decide which job you want now, we will ask the others what they want, and when you decide you can go to the job chart and write down your decision. If you haven't chosen by tomorrow I'll see what chore hasn't been chosen and write that down as your job."

Instead of:

> "I told you the bathroom was too big a job, but you insisted on taking it. Now you've left it half done."

try:

> "I can see that you feel you picked a very big chore for this week; however, I'm sure you will be able to handle it until the next meeting."

Instead of:

> "We've decided to go to the park this Sunday, so I'll shop for the food we'll need, pack the lunch, and get gas in the car. Is there anything else I should do?"

or:

> "Thanks for your offer to help grocery shop, sweetie, but I can handle it faster by myself and you can't carry the bags anyway because they're too heavy."

try:

> "Since we've decided to go to the park this Sunday, I will offer to make some chicken to take with us. Is there anything anyone else can think of that needs to be done?" As each item is mentioned, the leader asks, "Who would be willing to do that job?" If no one is willing, that part is left undone, or the leader asks, "What should we do about that?"

There is no one way or one best way to set up a system for doing chores. The goal of getting the work completed is secondary. The primary goal is to find ways for all members to feel they contribute to the welfare of the group and are needed, valued, and appreciated. No one in the family is merely a consumer but each is a producer as well.

We're interested in the process of communicating, sharing responsibility, and problem solving together. We're interested in teaching that all members are important and that there is dignity in the work each member does.

Issues and Concerns

The family meeting should be a gathering at which each member can receive help and can be of help to others. Help can be requested if a problem arises between any two members, or an individual member could also request suggestions with a personal problem. In order to give children the opportunity to develop and offer their own ideas, parents should avoid the temptation to give obvious answers too readily.

Six-year-old Katie brought up her problem of being teased by other children when she played with a boy she liked. Her nine-year-old sister, Sarah, offered a solution she had used, which had worked for her in a similar situation. She told Katie that she had refused to get upset. When the other kids asked her if she loved Owen or Andrew, she just replied, "Yes!" Sarah said when the kids could see that she wasn't getting upset, they soon lost interest in the teasing. Katie was pleased that her sister took an interest in her problems, and surprised to find that even her capable older sister had experienced similar difficulties.

It is also important that parents ask for suggestions or help so that children can see that their ideas are taken seriously and their opinions are important. This is an essential perception to develop for good citizenship.

The worst time to try to solve a problem is when emotions are high. When people are in the middle of a conflict they are more concerned with winning and/or hurting their opponent than with resolving the issue. Using an agenda can be an effective means for reducing daily bickering. Many families who hold regular meetings deal with everyday problems by reminding each other to put them on the agenda.

Placing an item on the agenda to be discussed later at the family meeting accomplishes a few goals:

1. It takes the problem seriously while removing the necessity of resolving it instantaneously.

2. It allows time for emotions to subside and people to back down from an angry stance.

3. It gives people an opportunity to evaluate their position and perhaps decide on a new direction.

4. It teaches that not all problems have to be solved immediately. In fact, many problems will have lost their urgency or importance by the time they come up at the meeting.

As the family becomes more experienced and adept at working together, even difficult situations that would normally be handled exclusively by parents can be handled by the entire group.

In one family, which gave out allowances during the family meeting, on the first of every month, Mother would place the entire monthly allotment into the "allowance can." At the end of each weekly meeting the children were given their share.

One day a neighbor held a garage sale and seven-year-old Kenny came home with lots of bargains. Several of the children in the family enjoyed Kenny's purchases, and one or two asked him where he had gotten the money, but no one pressured him for answers.

Mother stumbled onto the answer when she checked the allowance can and found approximately $8 missing. Her first response was anger, but she soon realized the money had not actually been stolen from her; therefore, it wasn't her problem to solve. This problem belonged to the entire family and particularly to the other children. At the next family meeting, when it was time to give out allowances, Mother explained that money was missing from the can. It didn't take very long for everyone to figure out who the guilty party was. Only one had shown evidence of new-found wealth. At first the other children were furious. They wanted their money back, but Kenny didn't have any money left. Next they turned to Mom and Dad and asked them to replace the lost funds. Although Mom and Dad agreed that the situation was not fair, they also reminded the children that the budget had already been allotted and there would be no more money until next paycheck.

Everyone began to give Kenny helpful hints on how he could replace the money. They suggested that he sell some of his toys, or borrow the money from friends or relatives. Soon they began to offer suggestions for helping him—perhaps they could hold a garage sale and put the profits back in the can. It became a family project.

The final result was less than hoped for, since the garage sale didn't net the amount they needed and the other ideas didn't pan out. The natural consequence of less money in the can was that each child had to take a proportionate cut in allowance until the next month when the family income was replenished.

If the parents had punished Kenny and replaced the money themselves they would have missed the opportunity to teach the children about responsibility and cooperation. The lesson Kenny needed to learn was that certain behaviors hurt others. Kenny was not a "thief"; he was a sweet little boy who made a hasty decision without thinking of the consequences. He was also a bright boy who decided not to do that again because he didn't like the results he got and he didn't like seeing others suffer because of him.

Happy Endings

Just as we began the meeting with compliments in order to foster a positive atmosphere, we want to end the meeting with an enjoyable experience. Therefore, many families end their meetings by planning a family activity for the coming week and sharing a special treat. Rotating the job of choosing and providing the treat can be an added honor and shows children that taking responsibility can be fun. This also ensures that everyone has an opportunity to get a dessert or a treat they enjoy.

Chapter 3

Meeting How-tos

Each family develops its own approach.

Leadership

A democratic society requires leaders as well as followers. Children in a democracy must be taught how to think for themselves and make wise decisions. Kids are often trained too well in following without being taught to choose whom and when to follow. Without good training in leadership children may look only outside of themselves for direction and follow others without question. These children are more vulnerable to peer pressure, cults, and even abuse.

The family meeting requires a leader or chairperson. The duties of a leader include:

1. Listening to others.
2. Recognizing all suggestions without judging.
3. Giving everyone an opportunity to speak.
4. Keeping attention focused on the topic that is being discussed until a solution is reached.
5. Summarizing conclusions to be reported in the minutes.

Although a parent may want to serve as chairperson for the first few meetings in order to provide a model for effective leadership, no more than a couple of meetings should occur before children are given their chance to lead. The chairperson role should be rotated weekly. The rotation schedule should be recorded in the Family Meeting Notebook.

The Record Keeper

Children six years of age and older can quickly learn to do simple recording of the date, names of those present, issues discussed, and solutions or decisions reached (see sample form in appendix). Even a member too young to write can take this job by summarizing proceedings using a tape recorder.

Families may find that a child who is known within the group as the "resister" becomes most cooperative when it's time to be the meeting chairperson. This child who doesn't like being told what to do may really appreciate the opportunity to show others that she or he knows how to be a leader.

Rotating leadership and record-keeping roles can have some unexpected benefits.

Peter was a thirteen-year-old foster child who had experienced some problems in learning. His reading and writing skills were very poor and he would try to hide these deficiencies whenever possible. One way he accomplished this was by refusing to run the family meeting or to be the recorder.

At one of the meetings someone asked if the meeting could be taped, and everyone agreed. When the children played the tape, Peter was able to see that he had spoken up quite often. He liked hearing himself, and when it was his turn to lead he agreed to give it a try. He enjoyed being the chairperson and he did a good job. Since the job of chairperson and recorder were rotated each week, it was time for Peter to be the recorder. He felt good about his leadership experience, but he didn't have the same confidence when it came to writing. The other kids told him he should take his turn and they would offer assistance if he needed it.

Peter did not attend the next meeting. He was down the street with his friends. One of the other children offered to read Peter's minutes but soon found this to be an impossible task. The meeting was at a standstill until someone went to locate Peter to tell him that he was needed to read his minutes. Peter was quite pleased. He too had some trouble figuring out his own writing, but as he pieced the information together, other members gave some assistance. When someone asked Peter to explain the first line of his writing, he said, "Oh, that one is easy. It says, M.R.M. That means Matthew ran the meeting."

Peter's development was different from that of the other kids. However, no one excused him from his responsibility, no one said that what he had to contribute wasn't needed, and Peter realized that his best was good enough for this job.

Guidelines

To obtain optimal benefit from the family meeting, certain guidelines are recommended:

1. A Specific Time and Day of the Week Should Be Scheduled for the Meeting. In order to affirm the importance of the family meeting, no change is allowed without the consent of all members. In this way the meeting becomes an integral part of the family routine.

Some busy families with ever-changing commitments find it difficult to meet on the same day each week. One solution to this dilemma is to add "choosing next meeting date" as a regular item on the agenda.

> HINT: Parents should show how important the family is to them by not taking telephone calls or allowing themselves to be interrupted during this "important meeting."

2. Everyone's Attendance at the Meeting Should Be Encouraged but Not Required. Every member is expected to come, since each one is an important part of the family. No one is forced to come, since coercion invites resistance and rebellion. No one is forced to leave the meeting, since that would be disrespectful to him or her. However, if someone is being disruptive, others may leave, thereby refusing to be disrespected.

3. Decisions Made at the Meeting Apply to Everyone Whether or Not They Attended. In this way individuals soon realize that it is in their best interests to have their opinions heard.

4. All Decisions Made at the Meeting Are in Effect Until the Next Regular Meeting. This rule teaches an important principle: that when we make an agreement with others it is a form of commitment to those others. If we don't like that agreement we cannot simply refuse to follow it or change it by ourselves. We are still obligated to live up to our commitments until everyone involved agrees to make a change.

5. The Duration of the Meeting Depends on the Ages of the Children. For young children, twenty to thirty minutes will probably be the limit. As children grow older and schedules change, each family can decide together what works best for them.

6. Decisions Should Be Made by Consensus. By using consensus instead of voting we develop group solidarity and teach cooperation. When decisions are made by majority rule, factions are likely to develop, and competition divides the group. People who don't agree with a rule and feel pressured to follow it may decide that others are unfair and excuse themselves from complying. Many problems arise when family members polarize along the lines of parents versus kids or males versus females. A simple example may suffice:

> Karen decided that it would be nice to have a little sister or brother. She brought it up at the family meeting. Dad, brother, and Karen voted yes but Mom voted no. Although the majority liked the idea, it was quite obvious that the veto carried deciding weight.

Consensus encourages cooperation and active participation. It demonstrates that, no matter how difficult the problem, if we persist we can come up with a solution that will be acceptable to all. This does not mean that people will always get their first choice, but they may get their second choice, or at least an *acceptable* alternative. If we cannot reach agreement, we put off making a decision until we can come up with a solution that is mutually satisfactory.

7. Discussion of Some Basic Rules for the Family Meeting Should Be Agreed Upon by the Group. Two simple rules, which have proven to be useful and effective, can serve as guidelines for all activities related to the meeting. First, the family meeting is a gathering at which all agree to respect themselves and each other. Second, everyone agrees to help each other.

Since family members may have different ideas about the definition of respect or being helpful, it is important to develop a "family definition." For example, respect could mean: attacking problems—not people; not putting others down; and allowing one person to speak at a time.

These two rules become the criteria for appropriate behavior and are useful in dealing with some common pitfalls.

If a suggestion is given that sounds sarcastic, unfriendly, or insulting, the chairperson may ask, "Do you think that suggestion will be helpful?" or "Do you think that suggestion was respectful to Diane?"

The chairperson can eliminate personal judgment from the response by addressing the person who received the comment, and ask, "Diane, do you think that suggestion will be of help to you?" or "Diane, did you feel respected by that solution?" If Diane is asked directly, she gets a chance to say how she perceived the suggestion. The receiver's perceptions are more important than the observer's perceptions.

8. Parents Should Make Sure They Don't Talk Too Much. Parents sometimes rush in too quickly with solutions and/or easy answers. Holding back gives others an opportunity to formulate and share their ideas.

9. Parents Should Also Avoid Rushing In to Protect One Child or to Stop a Disagreement for Fear It Will End in Conflict. Although the protection might seem to be a good idea, the one who receives the protection might interpret that response as a lack of confidence in her or his ability to solve problems. They may even feel insulted by the person who tries to protect them.

10. Don't Seek Perfection in the Outcome of the Meetings. Its purpose is to improve family life, to communicate with each other, to celebrate and value each person's uniqueness, to model values, to cooperate, to share responsibility, to teach the importance of helping others, to build self-esteem, to connect with each member, and to see how fortunate we are to have each other.

Chapter 4

Problem Solving

A forum where all problems, large amd small, are taken seriously.

Today's society holds many dangers for our children. Newspapers are full of stories about kids faced with abuse, drugs, alcohol, sexual activity, and violence. Children must be taught how to make wise decisions and to think for themselves. Without this knowledge kids are more vulnerable to yielding to peer pressure, to joining cults and gangs, and to being taken advantage of by unscrupulous adults.

Kids must also learn to take responsibility for their actions.

They should not be able to excuse their behavior by blaming others: "It was her idea!" "He made me do it!" "They told me I should!" "I was only following orders!" or depend on others to think for them or protect them from dangers: "You should have told me before." "I thought he knew how to drive." "I thought Joannie had asked her mother to pick us up."

Consequences Versus Punishment

Since we cannot protect our children from life, we must try to teach them to deal with it effectively. We must give them the opportunity to experience the consequences of their actions and to learn from their mistakes. Lecturing and warnings only turn kids off and make them think that the only danger to avoid is being stuck in a room alone with an "overcautious" adult.

Punishment too can backfire. When we arbitrarily apply an unconnected punishment, we run the risk of interfering with the learning process. The child may be so angered, hurt, or distracted by our reaction that he or she misses the real lesson: that his or her misbehavior is inappropriate, dangerous, or ineffective. This child may learn instead that he or she shouldn't misbehave because it gets us mad or that misbehavior is okay as long as you don't get caught.

Think of a time when you really got into trouble. What do you remember about it? Most people remember more about the punishment or the unreasonableness of their parents' reaction than they do about what they did wrong. The lesson children learn should always underscore the connection between their behavior and its results.

To this end we make a distinction between punishment and logical consequences. We define punishment as an arbitrary consequence, designed to teach through discomfort or pain, either physical or psychological. It works on the assumption that children learn best by *suffering* the consequences of their behavior. Consequences, on the other hand, work on the assumption that children learn best by *experiencing* the results of their behavior.

This does not mean that we allow our children to stumble into dangerous situations. We must always keep safety first, but whenever possible the parent should step back or arrange situations so that the child experiences reality. Respectful guidance allows children to experience safely the natural and logical consequences of their behavior whether they are positive or negative.

Thirteen-year-old Todd was playing ball in the backyard when a wild pitch broke a window. While Todd had not intended to break the glass, he had been irresponsible about playing so close to the house. Dad had a choice about whether to get angry about Todd's thoughtlessness or to solve the problem.

Yelling or other forms of punishment would have very little positive effect. Todd probably would have felt misunderstood and unfairly treated. Dad decided to take this as an opportunity to do some teaching.

The first thing that Dad did was to tell Todd how he could safely clean up and dispose of the broken glass. The next thing was to help Todd cover the broken window. Finally, since the broken window was a problem for the whole family, the issue was placed on the agenda for the next family meeting.

Although Todd didn't mean to break the glass, the monetary consequences of repairing the damage still had to be addressed. Todd was not blamed for what he did and he was not excused from taking responsibility for repairing the consequence of his behavior. The family discussed possible alternatives and finally agreed that Todd could decide whether he wanted to pay someone to repair the window or learn to fix it himself and pay only for supplies. Todd was also given the choice of using his allowance and savings to pay for the glass or doing additional house or yard jobs to equal the cost.

Todd decided that he would like to learn more about house repair, and besides he was saving up for a new baseball glove. So Dad and Todd made a date to work on the project together. Todd learned how to measure the pane of glass for replacement. Together, they went to the store and purchased the supplies for installing the new pane. Dad taught Todd how to remove the old putty, explained the rest of the steps necessary, and then they did the work together.

The major differences between consequences and punishment are:

	Logical Consequences	Punishment
Teaches	Cooperation, self-discipline	Arbitrary power, external control
Adult's emotion	Friendly, concerned	Angry
Adult's action	Seeking agreement related to behavior Thoughtful, deliberate	Hurting, arbitrary, often impulsive
Adult's focus	On the future (what needs to be done) On what *can* be done	On the past (what happened) On what *can't* be done
Child feels	Capable, respected	Belittled, inferior
Child remembers	Personal contribution Connection between behavior and results	Injustice, humiliation
Purpose	Self-control	Control over others

A logical consequence must pass the test of the Three Rs. It should be:

1. *Related* logically to the misbehavior. Instead of losing television privileges for missing dinner, you go hungry or cook and clean up for yourself. Instead of being grounded for breaking the window, you repair it yourself or pay for it out of your allowance.

2. *Respectful.* It should avoid any humiliation, and be both firm (to show respect for self) and kind (to show respect for the child).

3. *Reasonable.* It should be as logically understandable to the child as to the adult. An overly harsh or angry consequence is always perceived as a punishment.

Anger isn't necessary for effective problem solving. It only becomes necessary during a battle when someone feels defeated and wants to win.

Fail-Safes

A fail-safe is a previously agreed-upon consequence that states what each party can do if another does not hold up his or her part of the agreement. Using this concept for all persons involved allows consequences to be developed even when the child is in a strong battle of wills with the parent. This technique gives control over the situation to both parent and child. As children come to realize that they have self-control and some power over what happens to them, their need to demonstrate control by overpowering or resisting others will diminish. When there is a process for problem solving that respects all parties alike, even difficult situations can be addressed.

David and Hope came to a parent study group because they were so discouraged about their son, Rick. Although Rick was six years old, he was still soiling himself several times a day. He used the bathroom to urinate and never had an accident at school, but he continued to have bowel movements in his pants when he was with the family. Hope and David had tried everything from bribing to punishment in order to get Rick to stop. They were desperate. Nothing had worked. When they learned about fail-safes at their parenting class they decided to give them a try.

David used a family-meeting discussion about an upcoming canoe trip to try out what he had learned. He knew it was important to discuss fail-safes at a neutral time when people weren't angry and everyone could work together to solve a common problem.

DAVID: Rick, I've really been looking forward to our canoe trip but I have a concern I'd like to discuss. When I remind you to go to the bathroom, you get angry. I guess you feel disrespected. Is that so? (Rick nodded yes.) And I feel disrespected and angry when I have to put up with the smell of your messes. I would like to see if we can come up with another way to deal with this problem. Do you have any ideas?

RICK: Yeah, hold your nose!

DAVID: Well, I could do that, but it would make it hard for me to paddle the canoe, and anyway I wouldn't feel so good about that solution. Any other suggestions? (Rick shrugged his shoulders.)

DAVID: How about if I just butt out and let your poop be

your problem? If you need to go to the bathroom you tell me to paddle the boat to shore.

RICK: Okay, that's fine with me.

If everyone agrees to an arrangement, the discussion can move on. If an agreement is not reached, options are discussed until everyone is satisfied.

DAVID: We have an agreement—you'll decide when it's time to go to the bathroom and I won't remind you anymore. But what happens if one of us forgets?

RICK: No problem, Dad, I won't forget.

DAVID: Well, probably not, but since we both forget sometimes, one of us may slip up. Can you think of anything you could do if I start nagging you?

RICK: What do you mean?

DAVID: Well maybe you could think of some funny way of helping me to remember.

RICK: I got it, I'll tip the canoe!

David thought that this was a pretty creative solution and didn't mind the idea of an afternoon dip. No one should agree to anything that feels punitive, dangerous, or disrespectful. What's funny to one may feel like punishment to another.

DAVID: Okay, now we've got a fail-safe for me, and I'm going to be real careful not to slip up, but what about if you forget? What can I do if you smell bad and it bothers me? Would it be okay with you if I just paddled over to the bank and waited till you handled your business?

RICK: Okay, but remember no talking!

Rick was so anxious to catch Dad "reminding" that he was extra careful not to mess up. Both father and son were extra careful that day. Since both felt respected and both enjoyed the playful challenge, they had a good time.

At the next family meeting David and Rick discussed their trip and their fail-safes. Both agreed that it was a good idea. Rick felt proud of his ability to control himself, and he and his father were pleased that they were able to have a pleasant day without nagging or fights. They decided they would use fail-safes again in the future.

Whenever a fail-safe is used, the parties involved should be sure to make a date to evaluate the effectiveness of their choices and decide together if they want to continue to use them.

Common Mistakes

One way for parents to destroy the effectiveness of consequences chosen by the group is to get angry when someone applies the consequences to them. The family group should agree that the consequences are for everyone. If parents think they should be exempted from the rule, the kids will see that the meeting is one more way to control inferiors instead of a place where problems are solved.

The Bell family decided on an unusual fail-safe for helping people remember chores. Everyone agreed that they would be willing to be reminded if they forgot to do their chores. The only hitch was that they would be reminded at an inconvenient time and would have to stop what they were doing and immediately complete the chore. After a few interrupted television programs and several after-bedtime reminders, the children became very responsible.

All worked well until the long-awaited day when Dad forgot to do one of his chores. The children excitedly set their alarm clocks for an hour past Dad's bedtime. With great enthusiasm they awakened Dad and reminded him that he had forgotten his job. Dad was not amused, and he refused to follow through on the agreed-upon fail-safe. His refusal blew a perfectly good solution. The children were soon forgetting their chores again and no longer trusted agreements made at the meeting.

Children may change their minds about following the agreed-to consequence by claiming, "That's not fair. That is punishment!" If the consequence is reasonable and related, the parent may respond, "I don't see this as punishment, but as a way of *refusing to allow you to punish others by forgetting your chores!* I don't want you to be disrespected and I *also* don't want you to disrespect others. We all agreed to this at the last meeting. If you want to change that agreement let's discuss it at the next meeting."

Conflict Resolution

The encouraging and cooperative atmosphere of the family meeting provides a safe setting for problem solving. Using the following guidelines provides a useful structure for resolving conflicts:

1. Agree to respect each other. This means that everyone is entitled to express his or her own point of view without fearing attacks or put-downs.

2. Define the problem positively. Make sure everyone agrees that it is fairly stated.

3. Identify goals you have in common, e.g., "We all want to be able to have a good time together." "We all want to feel we haven't been taken advantage of." "We all want to have enough time to enjoy ourselves."

4. Agree to stick to the issue. It's easy to get sidetracked by bringing up past mistakes and behaviors, sharing negative expectations, and changing the subject. The chairperson is responsible to keep everyone focused on the current concern.

5. Express your position and feelings honestly and listen carefully to one another. Clarify with feedback: "From your point of view the situation looks like this:_____; and from my point of view it seems like_____." "It sounds to me like you feel_____."

6. Brainstorm possible solutions. To avoid a win/lose atmosphere of my idea versus your idea, come up with at least three alternatives. When choices are limited to two, polarities are seen—right/wrong, good/bad, smart/dumb. When a third choice is seen, other options become clearer. Any solutions that seem like punishment should be removed after brainstorming is over.

7. Evaluate the alternatives together. Decide what you will try. Be sure to develop fail-safes for what will happen if the agreement is broken or someone doesn't follow through (not a punishment, just an action that everyone agrees is respectful to all).

8. Set an evaluation date to see if there has been progress or what changes need to be made. The next family meeting is usually a good time for this.

If the group gets stuck at any step it's best not to force a resolution. Satisfactory agreements may take time to develop. A temporary measure can be used until the next meeting, when conflict resolution resumes. Sometimes a brief break clears the air and gives people a chance to reevaluate their opinions.

The meeting can easily be misused and undermined if parents fall into the trap of solving problems themselves and then using the meeting to convince the children they they should go along with adult solutions. Parents and children should be able to work toward solving short-term problems without losing sight of their long-range goal of establishing an atmosphere that fosters understanding and unites the family.

Chapter 5

Pitfall Prevention

One safely structured experience is worth a thousand lectures.

Many children are not allowed to experience the most basic of natural consequences. If a child forgets a lunch, mother brings it to school. If a child forgets homework, the teacher reminds or gives another day to remember it. If a child accidentally breaks something, some adult says, "Don't worry about it." When adolescents are caught drinking by the police they are usually given a warning. We give so many second chances that our children never know when we really mean what we say.

Some children reach adulthood still expecting someone to excuse them from responsibility and give them another chance. When the last chance comes, they are quite shocked. We will have to put natural, social, and logical consequences back into our home and school training so that our children are not deprived of the opportunity of experiencing the outcomes of the behaviors they choose.

Demonstrate Respect

When parents chair the family meeting they can model respectful behavior by remaining friendly and firm. In this way children learn how to:

1. Listen to Others. When one person interrupts another, the parent can be respectful while refusing to allow others to be disrespected, by saying something like, "Excuse me, Sandy, I'm interested in what you have to say, but I don't think Mike was finished. If he is, you're next."

2. Disagree Without Fighting. If someone becomes negative during a brainstorming session, parents can help to redirect the disagreement by reminding people of the goals of the discussion: "I can see we all have different ideas about handling this matter. How many would rather solve the problem than just fight about whose idea is best? It feels good to have several solutions. Why don't we list all the ideas we can think of. Then we can see if there's one idea we could all get behind."

Family meetings are not for arguing. Families argue every day. The purpose of the family meeting is to change that pattern. Fights often occur when people try to show each other what they are doing wrong. It's easy to see what others do wrong. We don't often see what we could have done differently. When blaming begins, the chairperson can interrupt the fight and ask everyone what they are willing to do to improve the situation.

3. Respect Other Members and Themselves. When someone seems to be looking for a disagreement or is simply enjoying the power of resistance the parent can firmly and kindly reveal what is going on.

> PARENT: Jeffrey, it looks like the only fun activity you will agree to is one that costs more money than we have to spend this week. We all want to have some fun together, so we don't want to disrespect you by choosing an activity against your wishes.
> JEFFREY: Great, then agree with my choice.
> PARENT: Well, I'm faced with a dilemma. It looks like I have to either fight with you and insist on my way, which seems disrespectful to you, *or* I have to go along with your idea, which costs more than we can afford, which feels disrespectful to us. I feel stuck. Could you help with finding a solution that doesn't feel disrespectful to anyone?

Consistency

One of the most common errors parents make is giving way to expediency (forgetting about a consequence because it is inconvenient at the time). Consistency is even more important when it is inconvenient. Without it we produce "testers," who keep pushing the limits to see if they can get away with "it" this time.

> Julie and Jim would often misbehave when the family went out to dinner. Their parents would yell and threaten to take them home, but since it was so inconvenient and the meal

had already been ordered, Mom and Dad never followed through.

The family had been invited to a fancy wedding, and Dad began to worry that the children's bad manners would be an embarrassment. When he stopped to think about what he could do to change the kids' misbehavior, he realized that it was his behavior that might have to change first.

At the next family meeting the parents brought up their concerns. They told Julie and Jim that the idle threats made by Mom and Dad had been disrespectful to the children. Mom said that she was sure the kids could behave appropriately, but if there was a problem in the future the family would have to leave the restaurant immediately. Julie and Jim promised that it wouldn't happen again.

The next time they went out to eat the kids waited a little longer before they started to misbehave. But, by the end of the first course, the old behavior patterns began. Dad said, "I see it's time to leave." Mom and Dad realized how much the children counted on the parents' inconsistency when Julie said, "But, Dad, that's not fair. You didn't give us any warnings! We didn't know you really meant *no* fighting!" This time the agreement was kept and the family left the restaurant.

Ask yourself, "How many times do I say what I mean before I mean what I say?" Your kids always know.

Sharing the Limelight

While some families worry about getting members to participate, other families complain about overly enthusiastic or controlling members who monopolize discussions. When one person does all the talking, other participants may get discouraged or bored. Putting this concern on the agenda can raise people's awareness and generate some interesting solutions. One family used a timer to limit each person's talking time. Before speaking, each person set the clock for five minutes. If the buzzer sounded it was time to let another person speak.

Involving the Resister

When one person consistently refuses to agree on any solutions or will only go along with his or her own suggestions, the problem of "roadblocking" may be put on the meeting agenda. In this way the resister becomes part of the solution.

Children who are not used to being included in the decision-making process may not trust that their opinions and wishes will be taken seriously. They may try to find out if they are right by refusing to participate. If they find that their views are really respected they will change their negative approach.

In one foster family Dad was an avid bowler and anyone who suggested bowling for the family fun activity was sure to have his vote. When Billy first came to this home he was suspicious when the foster parents told him that he would be an equal member of the family. At the first family meeting he decided to test this out by saying he didn't want to go bowling. This could have developed into an overwhelming pressure on Billy to give in to his new family so as not to make waves, but the family had a rule about consensus and lived by it.

It was wonderful to see this little boy's courage in speaking up for himself, and it was interesting to watch the other kids try to win him over during the week. They tried different selling approaches, telling him how great bowling was, and how great the snack bar at the bowling alley was, and they promised him that if he would try it once they wouldn't ask him to try it again unless he liked it. Without his vote the family fun activity could not be bowling that week. Billy realized that, even though he was the smallest and the newest member of the family, no one was going to force him to change his mind. In this home he was an equal and valued member.

Avoiding the Gripe Session

The family meeting is for problem solving, not for complaining and blaming. To discourage people from using the meeting as a gripe session everyone can be asked to suggest at least one possible solution for each problem they bring to the meeting. Some families emphasize the importance of this positive focus by calling this agenda item Problems/Solutions.

Don't let past failures serve as an excuse for not trying something new. Try saying to those who bring up the past: "I know you think Johnny didn't behave the way he should have, but is there anything you think you could have done to change the situation? I know the same old problems seem to be happening over and over again. What do you think would happen if we changed the way we respond to them? If we see a problem coming, is there something we could do differently before we get into trouble?"

Good Judgment from Poor Decisions

Parents may be tempted to jump in and warn children about ideas that might fail, or say, "I told you so!" when their advice is not heeded. If parents have all the answers children may not bother to think of their own solutions. This can set up a lopsided and disrespectful relationship, in which children have all the problems and parents have all the answers.

In order to help children develop their creativity and good judgment, parents should step back occasionally and let kids try different solutions (even ideas parents "know" won't work). Each week when the minutes are reviewed the family can analyze the results of their chosen solutions, talk about how things went, and decide what they may, or may not, do differently next time.

Families who use this approach often find themselves laughing together at the "good ideas that didn't work" instead of blaming each other and feeling discouraged about their mistakes.

No one in the Jordan family was willing to take the job of washing the dishes. The children didn't see why dishes had to be done daily. The group decided that they would each be responsible for cleaning up after themselves. By mid-week there were no clean glasses or silverware to be found. At first everyone blamed the others for not doing their share. By the next family meeting, however, the mess had reached humorous proportions and everyone agreed that they needed another solution.

Parent Traps

All new skills take training, and all beginnings have some difficulties. Even with the best intentions parents often fall into old patterns. Some of the most common errors parents make are:

- Too much talking
- Too much convincing
- Monopolizing the agenda with parental concerns
- Using the meeting to control
- Not taking the meeting seriously; i.e., taking phone calls or making appointments during scheduled meeting times

- Not following through on consequences or decisions made by the group
- Using parental privilege to excuse themselves from agreed-upon fail-safes or consequences
- Changing agreements without group consensus
- Trying to be *the* authority
- Having meetings only when problems arise
- Giving up when things go poorly

Chapter 6

Variations on a Theme
(What About Your Type of Family?)

LOOK, MOM, THEY'RE HAVING A FAMILY MEETING.

Different families have different kinds of meetings.

The Family with One Child

Only children live in a world of giants where everyone else can do things faster and better than they can. If these children are not given the opportunity to contribute and assume appropriate responsibilities, they may (1) come to enjoy this position with its special privileges and attempt to keep adults serving them; (2) become discouraged by comparing themselves to the grown-ups and decide that they are neither capable nor necessary; or (3) try to catch up with the adults and become precocious seven-year-olds going on forty! The only child may not learn how to negotiate or share (the give-and-take skills that become second nature to a child growing up in a home with other children).

All of these situations can be positively influenced by the introduction of the family meeting. Here a child can feel like a necessary member of the family unit, participating, sharing, negotiating, and solving problems. It gives the parent(s) a chance to see how the child's perceptions are developing and to determine what additional information or training might be necessary.

Two parents with one child may appear to the child as a united front making all decisions between them and handing down decrees. The child may feel that his or her opinions and contributions are insignificant or superfluous. This child especially needs a chance to feel equal and important. The family meeting's use of brainstorming, consensual agreement, rotating chairperson and recorder, and compliments minimizes the likelihood of this situation's developing and/or persisting.

Remember, an only child, like all other human beings, wants to feel connected, capable, and significant. In families where there are more than one child there may be numerous opportunities to find a place among equals. Parents of an only child must be sure to do what they can to arrange situations where these perceptions are fostered.

The Single-Parent Family

After the death of a parent or during separation and divorce, children are more likely to feel insecure about the future. The family meeting provides a chance for all members to air their concerns, support each other, participate in solving problems, hear about plans, and begin to experience themselves as people who are capable of handling the difficulties that life brings.

Single parents often find themselves in particularly stressful situations, in which they try to handle all of the family problems on their own. Feeling sorry for the child's loss, guilty about divorce and societal expectations, and/or pressured by a need to prove that they can make it on their own may lead them to overlook the fact that children are valuable resources. This oversight not only deprives the parent of necessary assistance, but it also deprives the children of the opportunity to feel like competent and contributing members of the family.

In some families a single parent may be relying too heavily on one or more of the children to handle the responsibilities of the absent parent. Many times an oldest child will happily take on more than he or she should in an effort to please a parent or feel important. This may keep the other children from feeling needed, included, and responsible. The family meeting encourages the participation of all family members and points out who does too much, who does too little, and what remains to be done.

The one parent–one child family may not think the family meeting is necessary for them. After all, they already have plenty of uninterrupted time together, and a formal meeting might seem contrived. However, anyone who has ever observed a real-life situation knows that the actual time spent discussing who does what, when, and why is minimal. When two people are alone they may forget about the importance of checking things out with each other. They may assume that they know what the other is thinking and feeling. If one is unhappy with a situation, he or she may be reluctant to discuss it openly, since the other hasn't complained.

The family meeting is a special time specifically set aside to address the problems and concerns of living together. It requires that all family members take the time out of busy schedules to sit down, face to face, and talk over the issues of everyday life, appreciate each other's strengths and contributions, plan for the coming week, inform each other of personal schedules, and decide what each will do to share the household tasks.

The Stepfamily

Stepfamilies come in all shapes and sizes. Some have one group of children with shifting parents; some have two groups of children who have to form a new group; some come together only for weekends, holidays, or summers; some have one group of children who are living in the home and another group of children who visit; some have children of two different age groups; and some with his, hers, and ours. There are so many varieties of step or blended families that we can't possibly name them all here. One thing they all have in common is that an already established relationship will have to shift in order to accommodate one or more new people.

Forming this new constellation may be confusing and distressing for all, owing to the loss of exclusive relationships; disagreements about rituals and the way things should be done; concern about loyalty to the absent parent; residual anger from the dissolution of the original family unit; loss of what they had (income, friends, toys, space, schools, extended family, etc.); changing parenting styles; disorientation about new roles in the family (oldest becomes second oldest, youngest becomes a middle child, little prince or princess becomes just one of the kids, "star athlete" becomes junior varsity member). The family meeting can be a critically important tool for facilitating this difficult transition.

By setting up a regular meeting, the parents can demonstrate how important working on this new family unit is. Building relationships takes effort, commitment, and time. The family meeting provides a respectful place for all family members to air their concerns, hear other viewpoints, and experience their significance and value to the overall group. Through discussion of chores, room arrangements, free-time activities, and the "way things are done," family members get to know each other better, commonalities may be discovered, and new alliances may be formed. Without the meeting, disappointments and disagreements may go underground and fester, or sides may be taken, with parents and siblings pitted against each other. For stepfamilies, as for all families, the family meeting is a preventive as well as a curative tool.

The Foster Family

When foster children come to live with a new family they will understandably feel disconnected, disoriented, and uncertain about the rules and rituals of the household. These are often kids who have been disrespected in many ways. Some have experienced neglect or abuse, and many have been shifted from one home to another without ever feeling that they really belong. These children may come to see themselves as unwanted, unimportant, and without rights. When these children enter a home that holds a weekly family meeting, they are immediately confronted with a new experience. Within no more than six days they will see that in this home their opinions are solicited and valued. As time goes on they begin to see that this is a safe place to express their concerns and trust in other people.

Some problems that foster families experience include fights between foster and biological children, perceived favoritism, insider-versus-outsider status. Foster children may fear expressing their wants or needs, since they expect to be ignored, ridiculed, or even punished for expecting too much. They may be afraid or unable to communicate openly.

Foster families need ways to build and maintain relationships with children who belong to someone else. They need a model for equality so that favoritism can be avoided or corrected.

The Extended Family

Families who have grandparents, friends, or relatives staying in the home, or live-in child-care helpers, may wonder about including them in the meeting. We have found that the family meeting is invaluable for solving the many daily issues that arise whenever two or more people are living together. This is a nonthreatening time for discussion, planning, and distribution of responsibilities. The necessity of contribution and cooperation from all household members becomes obvious. No one is too old, too insignificant, or too privileged to participate.

Anyone who is living in the home on the day of the scheduled meeting is invited to attend and participate. An overnight guest (child or adult) is invited to sit in on the meeting, since this is a way to introduce others to the concept. Many times people who have been invited to sit in on a family meeting have found it to be an extremely meaningful experience. We periodically get letters from relatives and friends commenting on how much they enjoyed participating in our family meeting. Our children and baby-sitters have, on occasion, requested permission to invite friends to our meetings just for the opportunity to experience the warmth and excitement of a group working together or to help the friend to work out a personal problem.

The Family with Very Young Children, No Children, or Fully Grown Children

The family meeting is not just for the children. It is important whenever two or more people live or work closely together on a regular basis. In any close relationship difficulties and misunderstandings are bound to arise occasionally. Many times one person is too shy or too embarrassed to bring up his or her concerns. Issues may linger below the surface, resulting in resentment and discouragement. Having an agreed-upon time to discuss any matters of concern encourages open discussion and communication, and points out the responsibility of each for interpersonal relationships.

The family meeting is for everyone. It provides a forum for addressing all kinds of concerns. Problems can be discussed and solved without bitterness, anger, or fear of retribution. This is a gathering at which all members have a say, are needed, and share responsibility for the outcome.

PART II

Encouragement

Chapter 7

Developing Self-Esteem

French and Latin students know that *cor* or *coeur* means "heart." To encourage someone is to put "heart" into that person. Courage is the quality that all people need if they are going to meet life's challenges. It is courage that helps children pick themselves up and try again, even though they may fail. It is courage that motivates children to try new things, enter new situations, and make commitments. It is courage that helps children go forward and do what needs to be done, even if what's needed is not the way of the group.

When children, or adults, are discouraged, they behave in socially useless or unacceptable ways. If children believe that what's expected of them is beyond their ability, they may give up, get angry, blame others, or figure out some way to cheat. This discouragement is costly to others, since discouraged people either refuse to handle their share of responsibility (which others must then handle for them) or they interfere with the work that others are doing. Courage is the antidote for discouragement. It is not an ability that one either has or lacks. It can be developed and nourished.

The best place to start encouraging is at home, since this is where children begin to form their self-image. Kids hear what we say and watch what we do and come to conclusions about what they *should* be like and how they *really* are. The difference between this self-ideal and self-concept determines the level of self-esteem. If the gap between the self-ideal and the self-concept is too great, the self-esteem is low.

Intentions Versus Perceptions

Learning how to encourage children is often difficult because one child may be encouraged by a remark that would be discouraging to another child. If we were to say, "I'll bet you can bring that B up to an A next marking period," to a child who gets good grades on a regular basis, that child *might* feel the adults have just expressed confidence in her or his ability. If we were to make that same remark to a child who just spent a whole marking period doing what he or she considered the best work possible, we might see the child crumble before our eyes. Good intentions are not enough. Even when adults are sincerely trying, they often fail because they are trying to encourage what *they* value instead of what the *child* values.

A mother and her five-year-old daughter were clearing the outside table after a picnic. Mother observed Jennifer pick up the largest pot on the table and head for the kitchen, and said, "Gee, Jennifer, I don't know what I'd do without your generous help with clean-up." Jennifer calmly set the pot down and went off to play. Mother considered why her attempt at encouragement failed. She realized that while her goal was to produce a child who enjoyed helping others, her daugher was more interested in showing how grown-up she was. Jennifer might have carried the pot to the kitchen and returned for another if she had heard, "Gee, Jennifer, I had no idea you were getting so big that you could lift the heaviest pot on the table. How strong you are."

Perhaps you can remember a time when someone tried to help you out by pointing to a "character flaw," a mistake you made, or an incident you were hoping no one had noticed.

Can't you see that your shoe is untied? It's a wonder you haven't broken your neck.

Why are you so selfish? Give your sister a bite of your sandwich.

You're so slow! When you grow up no one will want to hire you.

Didn't you see that table? How clumsy can you be?

No wonder no one wants to play with you. You always want your own way. You're so bullheaded.

That's the wrong answer. I can see you didn't put much effort into this.

Why are you so stupid?

How did you feel? Although these people probably cared for you and wanted you to succeed, it didn't feel that way. It more likely produced feelings of embarrassment, inadequacy, discomfort, and even anger. A child regularly exposed to this kind of interaction may become discouraged, feel like giving up, or refuse to try again because the same result may occur.

Good intentions are important but we have to check the results we get to see if we were successful. We must look to see what the children value, and provide evidence for them that they are reaching their own goals. The family meeting provides us with just such an opportunity to regularly check out our children's perceptions.

In all of the following examples, the parents have good intentions, but the children are not necessarily learning what the parents think they're teaching.

Johnny has an important paper due on Monday and Mom worries that he will put it off, as usual. She starts reminding on Wednesday and offers to take him to the library. Johnny may

decide that it is Mom's responsibility to be sure that he gets his homework in on time.

get angry at her for telling him what to do and refuse to let her push him around.

decide that this is a good way to get back at her for not giving him the money for those new sneakers he wanted.

Mary has forgotten her lunch again. Dad takes the lunch to school and lectures her one more time about forgetfulness. Mary may

tune Dad out; he's always overreacting!

decide that it's not so bad if you forget your lunch; you just have to put up with a little yelling.

decide that it's no use, she's just got a bad memory, and stop trying to remember.

George spills his milk and cries. Mom tells him not to worry, and just get out of the way so she can clean up the mess. George may

decide that it's up to other people to fix his mistakes and all he has to do is feel bad (the training ground for guilt feelings).

decide that he's not good enough or capable, that others can always do things better than he can.

conclude that if you can't do something well right away, you shouldn't even bother trying.

Jean is playing with her doll collection when Jason grabs one of the dolls and its dress is torn. Jean punches Jason and Mother smacks Jean.

Jean may

decide that Mom loves Jason more than her because she's always protecting him.

decide that hitting is a good way to teach someone, but only if you're the boss.

decide that life is not fair and boys can get away with misbehaving, but girls can't.

Suzy is the apple of everybody's eye. She works hard, follows instructions, and gets good grades. Mom and Dad are always praising her and telling her how much they love her. They often hold her up as an example to her sister, Eloise.

Suzy may

decide that love depends on performance.

believe that she must be best to be good enough.

learn to look to others to find out how well she's doing.

depend on others' opinions to set guidelines for behavior (now she's pleasing her parents, but when she reaches adolescence, her peers' opinions will be the ones that count).

Eloise may

decide that she can never be as good or as smart as her sister so why bother.

decide that if she can't be the best "best" she'll be the best "worst."

decide that if she can't excel in school she might as well stop trying and put her efforts someplace that pays off, e.g., sports, friends, music.

If the families in the examples above had regularly scheduled family meetings, and had instituted some of the techniques we have already mentioned, many of these problems could have been avoided. Instead of reminding Johnny to do his homework:

Mom would have simply done nothing or she might have asked Johnny if he would like to schedule a time for her to be available to help him out (and then waited for him to come to her). Johnny, having experienced the consequences of not planning ahead, would have learned that getting his homework done on time was his responsibility.

When Mary forgot her lunch:

Dad would have done nothing but express sympathy for Mary's plight and ask her what she might do in the future to help her remember. Mary would learn that if you forget your lunch it's your responsibility.

When George spilled his milk:

Mom would have told George not to worry and then showed him where the sponge was. George would have learned that accidents do happen, and that he was capable of fixing his mistakes. He would also have learned something about cleaning up that he could use in the future. He might also have decided that his Mom thought that he was pretty capable and it was safe to try new things, even if he couldn't do them perfectly at the start.

When Mom heard Jean and Jason fighting:

> She would have done nothing, unless she felt there was a real danger. In that case Mom could have asked the children to separate until they felt ready to resolve their differences in a less violent manner. Jean might have put the problem of Jason's taking her things on the agenda, or Jason might have brought up Jean's hitting as an item for discussion. Jean and Jason would have learned that there were many ways of resolving their conflicts and that it was in their best interests to find a way to work things out.

When Suzy brought home an exemplary paper:

> Mom and Dad would have told Suzy that they were pleased to see that she was putting so much effort into her work and that she must feel good about herself. Suzy and Eloise would have learned that their parents cared more about their effort than about the final product. Both girls would see that they could work for improvement not perfection. If Eloise compared herself to Suzy, she would not find herself falling short, since she too could put in effort and improve. Neither girl would mistakenly believe that their parents' love depended on how well they did.

Developing Strengths

All human beings develop traits and characteristics to deal with other people, with life and its situations. Character traits are resources people have developed in order to cope and go forward. No human trait or characteristic can be labeled until it is *used* in some way. If a quality is used for the benefit of both self and others, it is labeled positively—"leadership." If a quality is used in such a way that it seems annoying or harmful to oneself or to others, it is labeled negatively—

"bossiness." What's the difference? The difference is how the trait is being used. When people are discouraged they use their resources incorrectly.

Misbehavior is the symptom or overt sign of discouragement. It points to a child's concern about how to connect, feel capable, and/or count. Adults distracted by the symptom often overlook the "disease." Children need to be in relationships with adults who can look beyond their misbehavior, understand their concerns, and identify their strengths.

Can you remember a time when you were a child and an adult pointed to a contribution you had made, expressed a belief in your ability, or let you know in some way that you had what it took to be successful. You may have experienced elation, confidence, motivation, even surprise, but definitely a warm feeling toward this person. Experiences like these make us want to try again so that we can produce the same results.

A person who believes in a child will point to her signs of leadership, not her bossiness, and to his sense of humor, not his sarcasm. Finding strengths is the essential ingredient of encouragement. If we fail to develop this ability to see the positive potential in what the child is doing, we may miss the opportunity to motivate and encourage.

This does not mean that the adult should pretend the misbehavior is really a strength. The art lies in gently offering a way to bring the behavior to the useful side of life. Instead of trying to take a skill away, direct that skill toward a successful result for the child.

If there's a child in the family who criticizes the way others dress, why not go to that child when you are selecting an outfit and ask for an opinion: "What do you think? Does this match?" or ask that child to read over a paper to find errors. There are lots of jobs that require the ability to "critique." This is a way to put a talent to good use.

Effective encouragement techniques must be developed for

each individual; encouragement requires more than a pat set of gimmicks. Take a moment to think about each member of your family. Make a list of each person's traits. List both positive and negative characteristics. Can you see how their so-called faults could be seen as strengths if they were using these traits in a way that would be helpful to others? When we feel angry or defeated by others, we label their traits in a negative way, for example:

stubborn	or	determined
bossy	or	leader
nosy	or	inquisitive
fussy	or	particular
sissy	or	gentle
submissive	or	trusting
tactless	or	truthful
talkative	or	friendly
rude	or	forthright
overinvolved	or	energetic
unmotivated	or	content
excitable	or	enthusiastic
flighty	or	spontaneous
foolhardy	or	courageous
angry	or	standing up for beliefs
cocky	or	confident
aloof	or	cautious
manipulative	or	able to influence others
disorganized	or	comfortable with ambiguity
sarcastic	or	having a sense of humor
lazy	or	able to relax

When people are discouraged, they use their resources to protect themselves instead of using them to reach out to others. An encouraged person uses humor to lift spirits, to relieve tension, to bring others closer. A discouraged person uses humor to put others down, to hurt them, or to push them away.

In order to change useless behavior, we need to change discouraged perceptions. We don't want behavior modification; we want perception modification. Encouragement changes a person's perception. Children develop a positive self-image when they believe that the adults in their lives have confidence in them and believe that they have what it takes to be successful human beings.

Chapter 8

The Art of Encouragement

In order to increase the likelihood that we can positively influence a child's self-esteem, motivation, and courage, we can do the following:

1. Look for Strengths. Identify a variety of skills. While academic strengths are important, so are mechanical know-how, social capability, artistic endeavor, athletic ability, creative talent, visual acuity, and so on.

> Thomas Edison's mother used to complain about the messes he made.
> Beatrix Potter's father thought she was wasting her time on her drawings.
> David Brenner's teachers were always trying to get him to settle down.

Be especially aware of family values, since these strong beliefs may lead one to overlook other strengths.

> Lily and Mary were the daughters of two writers. Mary, the younger daughter, was more interested in taking things apart than in reading about them. Her older sister, Lily, was a high achiever, excelling in academics, writing for the school paper and even having some of her poetry published.
> Mary, growing up in Lily's shadow and knowing what was valued by her parents, felt she wasn't very bright. Her parents agreed she needed an extra boost and placed her in

a private school. She continued to be discouraged and finally dropped out of high school.

Mary moved to another state and got a job in a clothing store. She later completed work for a high school equivalency diploma. Her fine work was soon recognized and she was promoted to assistant manager, and before long manager. As this success was experienced she felt encouraged to start some college night courses, and it became apparent that she was a mathematics whiz. College was followed by graduate school, and she even completed her doctorate. Mary always had this ability but no one had noticed. It wasn't that her parents didn't care, they had simply overlooked her strengths because they weren't what the family valued.

2. Show Faith in the Child. Parents must be aware of the strengths and good qualities their children have to use in the times when a child needs emotional support. It's easy to feel justified in berating a child who brings home an F on a test; however, that situation also presents an opportunity to express faith in the child. Consider the following example as a father turns a negative experience into an encouraging one:

MARK: Dad, I flunked my science test. I really tried but I can't do it. I'll never be a scientist.

DAD: I know how disturbed I get when I don't do as well as I would like. What do you think the problem is?

MARK: I don't know.

DAD: What does it take to be good in science?

MARK: You have to be able to remember a lot of facts.

DAD: That's true. Anything else? How about observations and coming up with possible explanations?

MARK: Yeah, you're right. I had to do all that for our last experiment, and I'm no good at any of that stuff.

DAD: Gee, Mark, it surprises me to hear you say that. I always thought you were good at all of those things.

MARK: What do you mean?

DAD: Well, when you got into dinosaurs you remembered every species and where they came from. When you got into cars, you knew every make and model. When you got into hockey, you knew every detail of every player on every team. As far as observations and coming up with possible explanations are concerned, I've never known anyone who was any better at solving mysteries than you. Every time we play Clue or watch a mystery on TV you figure out who did it before I do.

MARK: I never thought of it that way.

DAD: Well, Mark, sometimes it's hard to see how the skills you use in one area can be applied to another area, but I think you've got what you need to succeed in science. If you decide you want to give it another chance and I can do anything to help, let me know.

(It can be very discouraging to fall behind in school work. Sometimes tutoring may be necessary to help a child catch up or develop new approaches to learning.)

3. Make Every Effort to Eliminate Criticism. Give up the myth of constructive criticism. Uninvited criticism pulls one down, construction builds one up; putting those two words together is what the dictionary defines as an oxymoron—they don't fit together because they have opposite effects. Criticism is usually advice you didn't want and didn't ask for.

When we care about others we want to help them remove obstacles to their goals, but if we don't want our comments to be seen as criticism, we need to be sure that the person we are trying to help is interested in hearing our feedback:

"Joe, when you asked me to read your science paper did you want me to read it as your friend, or did you want me to look for errors that would affect the grade you get?"

This doesn't mean that in order to accept the person we have to accept everything he wants to do. We can state what we want without putting others down.

Instead of telling a child he is irresponsible, we could say, "When you don't come home after school and you don't call, I get worried because I don't know where you are."

Sometimes the way we put something or the choices we give are the most useful ways to teach.

"We all agreed to go out to dinner on Sunday. Should we get dressed up and go to The Inn or should we all put on our jeans and go for pizza?"

This phrasing allows parents to exercise their values about dressing to match the occasion or setting and also keeps the relationship intact.

If you do find that you have to criticize or point out a mistake, be sure to end on a positive note.

Instead of "You did a good job setting the table, *but* you forgot the forks," try, "Nice job! You forgot the forks, *but* you did remember the spoons, the knives, and the napkins."

Most of us have experienced the letdown when someone finishes their comments with a statement about how our job didn't quite measure up. Wouldn't it be nice if all the "yes, buts" we heard were to tell us something positive?

4. Look for the Logic Behind the Mistakes. Mistakes are often very logical—incorrect, but logical. Piaget cautioned us to "Become more interested in *why* a child answered as she did rather than *what* the answer was." Instead of looking for perfection, look for analyzing ability, critical thinking, good judgment, effort, improvement, how far the child has come, not how far she has to go.

> "Diane, when you wrote the answer to number three, what did you think the question meant?" After the answer is given, the adult could respond, "Oh, I see how you came up with that answer. What would you have answered if you thought the question meant . . . ?"

> "Mike, when you did that, what were you hoping your friend would do? Did it work? If that happens again, what will you do differently? Did you learn anything about your friend? or yourself?"

> When your child's room still looks a mess after he or she has supposedly cleaned up, you may be able to avoid an argument by asking, "When I asked you to clean your room, what did you think I meant?" If your child answers, "I thought you meant to hang up my clothes and make my bed." You can stop and notice what *was* done and then move on to mention the other tasks that you *assumed* your child would think of. It is probable, even highly likely, that children don't hold the same perceptions as adults.

5. Help Children Learn from Their Mistakes. When mistakes are made, focus on what can be learned from them.

"Thank you for telling me about the mistake you made and how the tablecloth got stained. Now, what do you think you could do to fix it?"

"I can see that you thought if you hit your brother he might give your ball back to you. Since that didn't work, can you think of anything else you might try? I could *make* him give it back, but that wouldn't help you in the future if this happens to you again when I'm not around."

"I'll bet you felt terrible when you got to school and realized that you'd forgotten your homework. What did you do? How did it go? What did you learn from this experience? What will you do differently next time? Sounds like a good/ interesting idea. I think it's great that you don't fall apart when things don't go so well."

The family meeting is not used to help family members avoid making mistakes, but to help everyone see that

mistakes are an important way to learn.
correcting the mistake is more important than the mistake itself.
most mistakes are not devastating.
mistakes can be used as an excuse to give up or as a chance to try again.
making mistakes is the one prerequisite for being a human being; it's the one thing we can be absolutely certain that all humans do.

6. Give Positive Feedback. We do have to tell children what is unacceptable or inappropriate behavior, but we also have to tell them what we *do* like so they'll know. Be specific:

"I like when you did_____because_____."

"I liked the way you handled_____because_____."

"I liked it when you kept insisting your little brother take turns with you, because I don't want him growing up thinking he shouldn't be expected to cooperate."

"I liked watching you stand up to that teasing from the other kids. I'll bet they could see that you don't let them decide when you get angry."

"I like the fact that you don't fall apart when you make a mistake. There are so many things to learn that if we always worried about making mistakes we'd never get around to doing very much."

"I like that you come home on time. It makes me glad we extended your curfew because I can see that you're handling the responsibility that goes with it."

Appreciation time during the family meeting gives a regular opportunity to provide positive feedback.

7. Create Opportunities for Success. Divide up large tasks into lots of small ones. Instead of telling a young child, "Clean up your room!," ask him to pick up the big toys and say you will help pick up the small ones; ask her to pick up all the blue toys and say you will help pick up all the red ones; ask him to straighten the counters and say you will help with the dusting.

If the child spills milk from a large container, ask, "Would you like a smaller pitcher that would fit on the lower shelf in the refrigerator so that you can practice your pouring more often?"

Ask the child who has poor writing skills to make the

shopping list, so that the writing will be something that is needed, not just busywork that points to inadequacy. (The child whose handwriting is not so great could be asked to take the minutes of the family meeting.)

Don't produce artificial success because kids will usually see through it. One mom used to give her daughter credit for baking the bread or muffins when, in fact, she never allowed the daughter to help. The child felt doubly insulted. It was a task she had asked to do many times and she had been told she could "only" watch, and now she heard someone give her credit for having done it. Perhaps this mother was trying to encourage the child by giving her the credit for the baking, but it certainly didn't feel meaningful to the child.

8. Don't Feel Sorry. Feeling sorry for the child is also dangerous and disrespectful. If we feel sorry for children they may come to feel sorry for themselves, thinking that we believe they cannot handle situations. We can empathize with their plight but not excuse them from experiencing the consequences of their actions. While feeling sorry about a situation may be considered supportive, feeling sorry for a person is often experienced as discouraging and a vote of no confidence.

Five-year-old Jessica was an only child who was used to spending a lot of time with adults. After the first week of kindergarten she began complaining to her mother about how mean the other kids were and that nobody would play with her. Mother felt sorry for her little girl and tried to make it up to her with extra hugs, treats, and attention.

By the second month of school Mom was getting angry. She decided to go to school and see what she could do to help her daughter. The teacher suggested that Mom observe Jessica with her classmates. Mom could see that feeling sorry for her daughter had been a mistake and might even have added to the child's difficulties. Instead of joining in and cooperating with the other kids, Jessica would demand that the children play by her rules. When one child refused, Jessica said, "Well, I don't want to play with you anyway. My mom says you're not nice!"

The next time Jessica complained about the other kids, Mom responded differently. She acknowledged her daughter's feelings by saying, "It sounds like you really felt left out. That must have been hard. Do you have any ideas about what you could do the next time this happens?" Mom and Jessica discussed what makes someone fun to play with and Jessica came up with some ideas to try at school.

9. Don't Be Too Helpful. If we want to foster a feeling of competence and self-esteem in our children, we must create opportunities for them to develop skills, take on responsibility, and be accountable. Since we cannot protect children from life, we must prepare them for it.

When parents are too helpful, children may get the mistaken idea that their parents don't think that they are capable enough to handle life's requirements. Children may become discouraged if parents consistently excuse them from doing what they can do because the parents can do it faster, better, or more efficiently. These kids may give up trying to improve their capabilities and focus instead on improving their techniques for putting others in their service.

Alice was one of those fortunate children who had a "good mother" who was always willing to lend a hand. Mom would get up early and make Alice's lunch, remind her when her favorite television shows were coming on, and spend every evening helping her with her homework.

One night Mom told Alice that she wouldn't be able to help her with her homework because Mom had an important meeting to go to. Alice, always understanding and adaptable, replied, "That's okay, Mom, you can do it when you get home. It'll probably go faster if you do it by yourself."

Mom decided it was time to turn Alice's responsibility over to Alice.

We can only teach responsibility by giving it. All members of the family should be allowed and expected to contribute to the family through useful participation. As soon as a child is able to walk, he or she is able to begin to do small jobs.

Overprotection, too, robs children of initiative and courage. Some children may misinterpret the parent's concern as a message that "I must do it for you, since you can't do it up to my standards." These kids may decide that they just don't measure up, and begin to avoid all competition and situations where success is not guaranteed. Children need to learn to take bumps and rebuffs in stride. While a bruised knee will mend, bruised courage will remain a handicap for a lifetime.

10. Avoid Bribery. Using rewards as a way to get children to cooperate gives a very mistaken message. Instead of allowing them to feel the satisfaction of a job well done, the pleasure of contribution, or the gratification of helping another, we teach them to look for "what's in it for me?" As the children grow, so must the rewards, and if the reward isn't great enough, they may just decide not to bother. If an A in elementary school is worth a dollar, high school As are certainly worth ten, and a 3.5 college grade-point average must deserve a trip to Europe.

Matthew arrived home one day with a report card that he was proud to show. He asked if he would get some money for the As he had received. Mother said, "No, Matthew, we don't give rewards for good grades. You worked very hard for those grades and they are the result of your effort." Matthew declared, "Mom, that's not fair. Lots of my friends get five dollars for every A they bring home. How come you don't do that?"

Mom's answer: "Matthew, the reason we don't give rewards for good grades is that if we rewarded for the good ones we would also have to punish for the low grades. Rewards and punishments belong to the same system. You can't have one without the other. Dad and I believe that if you get a low grade you already feel bad and punishment from us wouldn't produce a lasting result. We also don't believe that rewards given for good grades will produce more good grades. In fact, we think it might actually take away the good feeling you felt when you saw your report card. The As you received belong to you, not to us, and we don't want to spoil your achievement by reducing it to some small amount of money."

"I'll tell you what we could do. Your brother and sister will be bringing their report cards home later this afternoon. Why don't we plan a little celebration tonight for all of you for having worked so hard during this marking period!"

11. Model Empathy. When people are afraid of failing or making mistakes or looking bad, they develop all kinds of ways to avoid the feelings of failure or not measuring up. When courage fails and good will is missing, we will see some signs of defensiveness. Parents can learn to recognize defensiveness as a possible sign of fear of failure. With this information they can pick up the clues that will help them identify how other family members perceive personal failure. It's not always easy to recognize defensiveness in others, but you will know it's there by the way *you* feel (annoyed, irritated, angry, hurt, resentful, despairing) in response to their behavior toward you. When we do notice this discouragement in others, we can encourage them by recognizing their feelings without excusing their misbehavior.

"I can see you're disappointed that I can't stop and play with you now. I have to finish this job, but if you like, I'll come and tell you when I'm all done and we can play the game then if you still want to."

"It feels like you're angry with me for not going along with your idea. I know you want to grow up and be able to make all your own decisions, and I want that too; *and* I also want to be sure that I don't excuse myself from handling my job as your parent. Maybe we can find ways for both of us to reach our goals in ways that don't offend each other."

"I felt hurt by what you just did (or said) and I know that people don't hurt first; they usually hurt back. I must have done something that felt hurtful to you. Could you tell me what it was so I can make sure that I don't do it again?"

"When you do that it looks like you would like me to leave you alone. I would like to be with you in some way that doesn't feel so full of pressure to you. If you think of anything I'd sure be interested in listening."

The real test of encouragement is to ask ourselves before we speak, "Is what I'm about to say going to make this child *more* willing to try or *less* willing to try?"

Many years ago Johnny Mercer summed up the art of encouragement with his popular lyrics, "You have to accentuate the positive, eliminate the negative, latch on to the affirmative, and don't mess with Mr. In-between!"

Family Meetings Build Courage

Many people talk about family meetings and use them for various objectives. Some use them to "lay down the law," some for "crisis intervention," and others as "a last resort." We use the family meeting as an important prevention tool, which also enriches the quality of family life. At the family meeting we can consciously model and teach the behaviors that we want to foster in our children. On a weekly basis we can encourage our kids and be sure that they experience all three Cs. By expressing and receiving appreciation and compliments, by asking and giving advice, by problem solving and the taking on of chores, children get to see that they are *connected*, they are *capable*, and they *count*.

The more involved they are in a cooperative atmosphere, the more they feel that they belong.

The more they feel that they belong, the more they feel like contributing.

The more they contribute, the more they feel responsible.

The family meeting is a place where everyone, together, helps each other to become a more effective member of the family and society. Children are then able to maximize their potential, since they have the courage and willingness to master the essential skills required for a successful and happy life.

PART III

Logical Discipline

Chapter 9

Parenting Styles

Parents are at a disadvantage. They take on the most important job that society has to offer with little training and no experience. In fact most people are so excited about having a child that they don't think about the how-to of raising one. Their lack of preparation doesn't become apparent until they're already "on the job." Under this kind of pressure most people resort to one of three things: (1) they do what their parents did, (2) they do just the opposite, or (3) they start off one way, and when that fails, they revert to the other way.

The three most common mistaken approaches to parenting are:

1. Laying Down the Law. Trying to *make* them conform or "do as I say," (or, as some parents euphemistically put it, "cooperate").

2. Pampering. Doing things *for* children and giving in to their demands.

3. One from Column A and One from Column B. Parent A tightens control to avoid raising a "spoiled brat" and parent B tries to make up for this "unfairness" by being extra flexible. Each parent may go too far trying to make up for the other parent's "mistakes."

In one family with four children, whenever one of the kids makes a mistake, Mom lectures, scolds, and explains in great detail what should have been done instead. Dad sees the looks on the kids' faces and feels sorry for them. He always rushes in to say, "They didn't mean to do it. It was no big deal. Why do you always overreact? They're only kids."

Mom is worried that her children aren't seeing that manners are required in society. She's also afraid that people will think she didn't do a very good job of teaching her kids. Dad is concerned that the kids will be so frightened of making mistakes they'll never try anything. He thinks they need to be rescued from Mom's high standards.

Why Not Lay Down the Law?

Some parents say, "Kids today have it too easy. Children should do as they're told. I listened to my parents and my children should listen to me." It might be nice if it worked, but laying down the law isn't effective either.

Parents today are rightfully concerned about the many dangers their children have to face. They want their kids to avoid strangers, even if they appear friendly; say no to drugs and alcohol, even if it means being left out; make responsible decisions about sex, even if their friends say "it's not cool." Parents who want to raise children who can use good judgment and think for themselves cannot afford to train them in blind obedience. A child who only follows orders does not learn how to make choices and develop judgment.

When children are arbitrarily forced, they feel put-down and have to figure out some way to maintain their self-esteem. Depending upon how powerful they feel or what options they see open to them,

they may fight, openly say *no!*
they may resist, passively say *no!* (by forgetting, dawdling, or using some other undercover technique)
they may say *yes*, and act *no*.

Laying down the law is dangerous because it does not teach cooperation. Coercion teaches that might makes right and that respect goes in only one direction—*up!* These children are not prepared to take their place in a society of equals. Instead, they see the world divided into winners and losers, wise guys and suckers, leaders and lackeys.

Why Not Pamper?

All of us are aware of the effects of child neglect and abuse and view both as a severe form of deprivation. *Few adults see that pampering is also a serious form of deprivation.* It deprives children of the opportunity to learn the skills they need to survive in the world. Pampered children are handicapped since they do not see themselves as obligated or able to take their places as equal members in society. They resent the feeling of dependency and, at the same time, see it as their right to be served. These children may get angry and even punish those who do not meet their demands. They, too, divide the world into superiors and inferiors, those who serve and those who are served. Cooperation and doing for others may be seen as signs of weakness and inferiority.

Parents may be confused. They've heard about the importance of modeling or setting an example of appropriate behavior and wonder why they're producing demanding tyrants when what they're trying to model is kindness and helpfulness. The answer is simple: parents have left out one important ingredient—self-respect. Although the parents respect the child, they forget to respect themselves. Since parents do not model self-respect, the children don't learn to respect them either. Children observe their parents' indulgent behavior and come to believe that this treatment is their right.

One pampering parent became aware of the extent of her daughter's mistaken ideas while preparing for a mother-child costume party. When Mom asked her eight-year-old daughter what they should go as, Joanie capsulized their situation in her response, "I know! I'll go as a rich lady and you can be my maid!" It dawned on Mom that this was "business as usual."

This mother was fortunate. She learned a valuable lesson while her child was still young enough to be influenced. By changing her own behavior, Mom was able to give Joanie the opportunity to learn about respect and the correlation between rights and responsibilities.

Some parents wishfully label their children's selfishness as "just a phase" they're going through. They hope that their children will automatically grow out of this stage with just a little lecturing and no substantial changes in their parenting techniques.

This was not the case for the mother who was overheard explaining to her friends why she was late for their tennis date, "I'm sorry I kept you waiting. My sons were running late this morning and I had to be sure they had their breakfast." She stopped and thought for a moment, and then added, "But I don't know why I worry—they usually eat when they get to the *office* anyway!"

Pampering is irresponsible because children do not learn what is expected of *them;* they only learn what they can expect from *others.* This will not change until parents stop providing undue service and yielding to unreasonable demands.

Firm and Kind

Rudolf Dreikurs said, "Freedom is part of democracy; but the subtle point that we cannot have freedom unless we respect the freedom of others is seldom recognized. . . . In order for everyone to have freedom, we must have order and order bears with it certain restrictions and obligations. Freedom also implies responsibility" (Rudolf Dreikurs, *Children: The Challenge* [New York: Hawthorn Books, 1964]).

Parents have an obligation to raise children to become responsible citizens. Children need to learn that true freedom can only exist within a social order. Without certain limits no one can feel secure, and without the opportunity for choice no one can feel free. Imagine how frightening it would be to cross the Golden Gate Bridge if it had no guardrails. Although we try not to bump into the railing, we feel secure knowing that it's there.

We must provide children with safe opportunities to make choices and experience the consequences of their choices. Our parenting techniques should combine the firmness and structure of the "Lay down the law" parent and the kindness and flexibility of the "Pampering" parent.

Twelve-year-old Jeff couldn't understand why Mom wouldn't let him go to a rock concert with his friends. He got so frustrated that he ended up calling Mom a stupid dope. Although Mom was hurt and angry she knew hurting him back wasn't the answer.

Later that afternoon Jeff came by to ask Mom for a ride to his karate lesson. Mom took this opportunity to teach Jeff about the consequences of being rude. "Jeff, I realize you need a ride to your lesson, but as your mother I'd be concerned about the safety of putting you in a car driven by a stupid dope."

Jeff quickly apologized and said he hadn't really meant it, that he was just angry before. Mom said, "I accept your apology, and although I'm glad you're feeling better, I still feel disrespected. I know it took you some time to calm down, and I'm sure I'll feel better by tomorrow. I'll be happy to help you out then." Jeff tried to get Mom to change her mind by complaining, "Mom, I said I was sorry and I can't miss my lesson." Mom remained firm and friendly, "I know your lesson is important to you but you'll need to figure out another way to get there this time."

Mom did not lecture, scold, or punish. She taught respect by refusing to be disrespected.

A respectful approach to discipline is both kind and firm; it replaces punishments and rewards with natural and logical consequences. In this way we refuse to abuse children through punishment, insult them through bribery, or interfere with their learning by protecting them from bumping into reality.

Chapter 10

Mutual Respect

The family meeting is a great opportunity to discuss what should happen if any family member refuses to keep the rules that the group has adopted. The family is trying to establish a social order that maintains a common logic—logic that everyone understands and sees as sensible, reasonable, and related to the situation. A logical social order allows any member (probably from age four up) who tests a rule to experience a known-in-advance consequence. When we know the rules in advance we have a choice and we don't experience the insecurity that comes from the unknown.

A consequence that uses social logic says, in effect, "I'm not interested in punishing you, *and* I won't rescue you from the consequences you choose for yourself (with the exception of dangerous or life-threatening situations), *and* I will ask you to respect me.

Some consequences that families have agreed upon at their family meetings:

Toys left out at bedtime will be put away for one day by anyone who must step over them.

Only those clothes put in the hamper or laundry room will be washed.

If items are left scattered they are placed in a box in the closet by anyone who wants the area neat.

If two people are arguing over television programs, the set will be turned off (by anyone who is disturbed by the argument) until an agreement is reached on which program will be watched.

If a person returns the car without at least a quarter of a tank of gas, it will not be loaned to that user for one week.

Doing Less in Order to Teach More

Logical consequences may be developed by an individual without taking an issue to the family meeting, especially when disrespect is felt (as in the case of Jeff's calling his mother a stupid dope) or in such situations as these:

Mother's jobs included table setting, but whenever she went to set the table she found it covered with everyone else's things. She got pretty tired of constantly reminding everyone to come clear off their belongings.

Mom finally tried a new approach. After all, she had chosen the job of table setting, not of family nag or chief reminder! She decided that she would stick to her bargain and just do the job she contracted for.

When the family arrived for dinner that night they were confronted with a funny sight. All the dishes and silverware were set on top of papers, books, and jackets. All could see that they would have to put their things away before anyone could eat.

While Mom laughed along with the others, she made it clear that this was no joke and that she intended to keep to this new routine.

Deciding not to fight, not to give in, and not to force the child into our way of thinking can have some surprisingly positive results:

Tom, a father fresh from a parenting course, was ready to handle situations in a new way with his eight-year-old daughter, Michelle. When Michelle presented her new dilemma—outgrowing her small two-wheeler—Dad was ready to deal with this in a friendly way and avoid their usual fights. He agreed with Michelle that her bike was, indeed, too small. Then she announced that she wanted the ten-speed model she had her eye on at the bike shop.

Tom was an experienced businessman and a good salesman, and so he used his best adult logic to try to convince her that the ten-speed was well beyond her basic needs. His offer was to purchase a three-speed bike that would suffice and was a much better buy.

All parents everywhere can predict the struggle that was about to occur. Michelle gave back her carefully planned eight-year-old's logic about why nothing but a ten-speed would do.

Dad was searching for a way to be a good parent without fighting or giving in, and so he told Michelle he wanted her to have a new bike. He had looked at the prices and was willing to give her the price of the three-speed, which he felt would meet her needs; but he had no intention of forcing her to purchase something she didn't want. He told her she still had some choices: she could consider buying a bike with the money he was giving her, or she could hold on to the money until she had enough saved to get a more expensive one.

Michelle decided to stick to her own ideas. This family lived in a rural area so work wasn't that easy to find; however, nothing would stop Michelle's enthusiasm. She contacted everyone she knew for odd jobs. She walked dogs, looked after pets, collected eggs, and asked for any job that was available. By the end of the summer Michelle got the bike she wanted. She was quite proud of her accomplishment and she wasn't the only one. Tom was very impressed with his daughter's entrepreneurial skills—a chip off the old block!

In this case Michelle chose to experience the consequence. It was more difficult than giving in, but it gave her an opportunity to feel respected and independent. If Dad had forced Michelle to see the wisdom of his ways or tried to *make* her work for the extra money, the experience would have felt like a punishment. They might both have missed this chance to see how capable, determined, and enterprising Michelle could be.

Rights and Responsibilities

To paraphrase the social psychologist Erich Fromm, the United States made a big mistake when it placed the Statue of Liberty on the East Coast and forgot to place a statue of responsibility on the West Coast. A successful democracy requires that its citizens know how to use their freedom and acknowledge their responsibility. Rights and responsibilities cannot be two separate issues.

Ben was seventeen and feeling good about his independence as an adult. He had a job in a fast-food restaurant and worked late some nights. His parents asked him to post a schedule so the family would know when to expect him. Ben posted the schedule, but when his coworkers invited him out after work on weekends Ben forgot about the schedule and came home very late. His parents then requested that Ben call home when he was planning to be with his friends so that they could change their expectations for his arrival and stop worrying about him.

More and more often, Ben began to call to say he would not be home by the agreed-upon time. The parents began to feel disrespected and unable to handle their parental responsibilities. They requested that Ben come directly home on the one school night he worked. On weekends, the time would be extended within a reasonable limit. Ben and his parents agreed on the limits.

The discussion revolved around the rights of parents and teens and the responsibilities of parents and teens. All agreed that parents have the right and the responsibility to set limits for being home on school nights.

Ben chose one more time to come home very late on a school night after all family members were in bed. At this point Ben's parents asked him to turn in his key, since he was avoiding his responsibility and infringing on his parents' rights as well. Ben was told that if he arrived home at the agreed-to time they would see his willingness to cooperate. If he arrived home by the time the parents went to bed (11:30 P.M.), he would still get in. However, if he chose to come in later than that, the door would be locked.

Ben was asked how he would handle this situation. He said that since a friend drove him home he would ask the friend to wait to see if the door was unlocked. If he was locked out he would spend the night at his friend's house. The parents would not have considered this option for a much younger child. Ben, however, was seventeen and one year away from independence. He needed to become more reliable and responsible.

Ben still continued to test the system. He came home again after the house had been locked and went to the window of a brother's bedroom, threw some stones at the window to wake him up, and asked that he be let in. His brother complied. The parents brought this up at the next family meeting and requested that all family members allow Ben to experience the consequences of his unwillingness to cooperate. They explained that Ben didn't have the right to disturb the sleep of others for his convenience. This was disrespectful, and one of the family rules was to respect self and others.

Ben tested the rules one last time, but since his parents remained friendly and firm he was able to see that he had lost one of his rights because he didn't accept the responsibility that went with it.

Freedom Within Limits

Our goal is to produce children who by the age of eighteen are self-sufficient and can live among others in a responsible way. In order to reach this goal, the child's freedoms and rights, as well as limits and responsibilities, should be expanded in accordance with the child's development and capabilities.

The following chart will give you a good idea of what is appropriate for each age group:

Age	Freedom	Limit
Under 5 Parent provides structure, safety, limits, rules	May go outside	Stay inside the fence
	Choose breakfast	Cold or hot cereal
	Watch television	"Sesame Street" or "Mister Rogers"
5–7 Parent gives more opportunities for independence and responsibility	Choose what to wear	From this rack for school From this rack for play
	Select hobbies and activities	If they are respectful to self and others If we can afford them
8–12 Parent begins teaching drug and alcohol prevention. (This is the best time after fully developed thinking and before puberty)	Select time for homework	After school, before dinner, or after dinner
	Select a way to contribute to the family	From a job list or in a way that the family agrees to

Age	Freedom	Limit
8–12 (cont.)	Decide when to do chores	Before dinner or before bedtime
	Choose friends	Invite them home to meet parents
13 up Child continues moving toward self-sufficiency and connection with adult world of responsibility	Choose bedtime	Be in bedroom by . . . No late showers or loud music after 10 P.M. on school nights
	Get driver's license	After satisfactory arrangements for insurance have been made
	Borrow family car	If arranged beforehand and the gas is replaced No drinking, no drugs

Logical Starts

Although we spent a lot of time talking about logical consequences, it is important to remember that such techniques won't always be necessary if parents anticipate problems before they arise.

Parents need to take the time to teach children to cooperate with the social order. The best time to teach a new skill or behavior is when there is time set aside for that purpose. We don't teach a child how to tie shoes when we're running late. We shouldn't teach children public eating behavior when we're headed for an expensive restaurant.

The family meeting is a good place to begin logical starts like teaching skills for handling jobs and preparing for an unknown (a doctor's visit, eating out, an airplane ride). Consequences are more respectful and easier to accept if we know what is expected of us.

When parents decide that it's time to teach the social requirements of public eating, they should be sure to take the time to discuss (and even practice) appropriate behavior. Parents should also stress the importance of being considerate of other people's rights. Everyone in the restaurant should be able to enjoy his or her meal without being disturbed. "When we go out we have a choice. We can enjoy a pleasant lunch as long as everyone uses good manners, or we can leave the restaurant and try again another time."

Parents may then select an inexpensive place to get a snack, and if the child misbehaves, the parent could say (firmly and friendly), "I see you've decided to leave," or "When you yell and cry in the restaurant it disturbs others who are eating. We will have to leave now." The parent then gathers everyone together and leaves. If the child complains or asks for another chance, the parent replies, "It's okay, we'll try again another time." There is no lecture, no recrimination, no punishment. We simply allow the child to experience a social consequence. If this procedure is followed consistently, it will pave the way for many pleasant restaurant experiences in the future.

Many parents will react to this solution by saying, "Why do I have to suffer the consequences of my child's behavior?" The answer is twofold:

1. Parents are obligated to train their children and lectures won't work. One safely structured experience is worth a thousand words.

2. Leaving a few dollars' worth of food uneaten once or twice is enough to teach a lesson that will allow the family to eat out for the next several years. That kind of training is worth the price for many parents.

Family Meetings Raise Children for a Democratic Society

Children of today must be prepared to live in the world of tomorrow. Rapid changes in technology and advances in knowledge have affected the way we think, feel, and act. Tradition and values are often lost in this fast-paced world. Under these circumstances parents have an even greater obligation to:

1. Help children learn the skills they need to survive and succeed in today's society.
2. Prepare them to take their places as contributing members in the world of tomorrow.

In this chapter we have described a system of logical discipline that is designed to help parents raise kids who can use good judgment, assume responsibilities, communicate effectively, respect themselves and others, cooperate, develop self-esteem, and enjoy life.

The family meeting is a natural complement to logical discipline. By committing ourselves to a weekly meeting, we ensure that our children have the opportunity to experience themselves as competent, contributing members of a family group and give them the opportunity to learn and practice all of the skills mentioned above.

It's All in the Meeting

The primary purpose of this book has been to show how the development of children's necessary perceptions and skills is facilitated by the family meeting.

Perceptions: The "Three Cs"

I am connected to this family; I feel that I belong.

The meeting provides a time for togetherness, a family ritual that is seen as important.

Each person is given the opportunity to identify with and take responsibility for the group process.

Each family member is guaranteed acceptance, a chance to be heard and taken seriously.

I am capable; I have what it takes to be successful, and I can influence what happens to me.

All members function as part of a working unit.

Each person develops self-esteem and confidence through hearing others point out strengths.

All family members get to share ideas and have those ideas considered and used.

Children see that mistakes are learning opportunities, not signs of failure.

I count; I can contribute in meaningful ways and I am genuinely needed.

All members participate in family discussions and decision making.

Everyone is listened to and taken seriously.

Each person shares the household chores and tasks.

Everyone is given the opportunity to help those who need it.

All are asked to take a turn at leading the meetings and taking notes.

All members get an opportunity to hear that others appreciate them.

Skills and Abilities

Communication

Everyone is given a chance to speak and to be heard.

Family members are taught how to listen and learn to respect others by not interrupting.

Everyone hears how others share ideas and feelings.

Cooperation, empathy, respect, and negotiation are modeled so that children learn how to communicate in ways that invite others to listen.

Good Judgment

The group discusses the significance of their experiences.

Problems are identified and analyzed. A variety of solutions are tried.

Solutions are examined to see if they are respectful to self and others and to see how they will affect each member.

Choices are given and consequences are experienced.

Responsibility

Everyone is given a chance to contribute to family life.

All family members are asked to take turns leading meetings, taking notes of the proceedings, and participating in nonleadership roles.

Choices, consequences, freedom, and limits are given to all.

Solutions are solicited from everyone.

Self-Discipline

Rules and consequences are decided upon by all.

All members get to experience the consequences of their actions.

Everyone gives and receives feedback.

Qualities

Courage

Recognition is given for effort and improvement.

Strengths are identified and talents are recognized.

Opportunities are given for people to learn from and correct their mistakes.

People are not labeled. Behavior is rejected, not the person.

Cooperation

Family members count on each other.

Each person's contributions are appreciated and needed.

Family unity is developed.

Like all techniques or tools, the family meeting is only useful if everyone feels the benefits. Some benefits are short range and some are long range. You may be tempted to stop the meetings when there seem to be more problems generated than the ones solved. Remember that you're trying to show kids that problems can be solved if you stick together—that it's normal to be discouraged or unhappy from time to time, but it's not okay to say that's the way it has to be. If you stop the meetings when there are problems, one child may feel that she or he is at fault, and others may get the idea that when solutions are not readily available it's okay to quit.

Life is full of problems and those who are successful in life are those who see problems as an opportunity to find solutions, not an excuse to give up. As time passes, review some of the minutes of past meetings and see what was achieved as a result of some decisions the group reached.

Our families have records from many years of holding meetings, and an added reward is the fun we have reviewing this chronicle of the ups and downs of our life together. Foster children and friends of the family who have experienced the meetings often ask on return visits, "Do you still have family meetings?" Each one recalls a few meetings that were particularly memorable.

In this world we are often confronted with the fact that nobody can do it for you *and* you can't do it by yourself. It is reassuring to experience the family as a gathering at which each member has some responsibility toward every other member, and each person can feel connected, capable, and significant.

Appendix

Sample Agendas

The Bettner Family Meeting Agenda

Meeting held on: Leader:

Members present: Minutes taken by:

Appreciations/thank-yous/compliments:

Last meeting's minutes:

Issues/concerns: Name:

   Issue:

   Suggestions:

   Solutions chosen:

   (repeated for number of issues presented)

Announcements:

Family needs for coming week:

Family jobs to be handled this week:

   Name: *Job selected:*

This week's family fun activity:

Next meeting time and place:

Refreshments (chosen or prepared by chairperson)

Family Meeting Agenda for Young Children

 Minutes from last week

 Appreciations/thank–yous/compliments

 Issues/concerns and solutions

 Announcements

 Family needs

 Family jobs

This week's fun activity

Drawings by A. Christine Polischuk

The Lonberg-Lew Meeting Format

One minute of silence: To think about compliments and appreciations.

Compliments/appreciations:

Review of old business: Reading of minutes by last week's recorder. Are solutions working? Does anything need to be readdressed or forwarded to next meeting?

New business:

Handling of concerns written on posted agenda

Announcements

Plans for coming week

Family finances

Box check: This is a fail-safe for clutter: Possessions left out for more than twenty-four hours are placed in a box and cannot be retrieved until family meeting. Everything in the box must be put away before treat is served.

Family treat: Provided by current chairperson with money from treat fund.

Adjournment at 8 P.M.: In order to participate in family ritual—"The Cosby Show."

Classroom Meetings

Can you imagine how successful each child could be if both parents and teachers used strategies that developed the "Three Cs," and taught essential social skills? Rudolf Dreikurs recommended that meetings be held at home and in schools.

Frank Meder, an elementary school teacher, and John Platt, a counselor, in Sacramento, California, developed an impressive system for classroom meetings.

Students are taught to list any problem or issue they have in an agenda book that is available for students to use. Each week, at a scheduled time, the class quickly forms a circle with their chairs and solves problems together.

The model uses two steps, compliments and problem solving.

Compliments

The teacher calls on anyone who has a hand raised and is willing to compliment another student or group of students. Students who receive compliments respond by saying "Thank you."

Problem Solving

Using the agenda book the teacher calls on the first person whose name appears in the book and reads the problem listed, followed by the question: "Jim, is this still important?" If Jim says, "No," the teacher goes to the next item listed on the agenda.

If Jim says, "Yes," the teacher continues by asking the class:

"How many people like it when this happens to them?"

"How many people don't like it when this happens to them?"

This quick tabulation is an instantaneous and powerful way to poll the group for its opinion on socially acceptable or unacceptable behaviors. Instead of feeling criticized by the teacher, a student is able to see how a behavior impacts on others.

If the complaint has been lodged against another student, that child is asked: "Susie, do you think something should be done about this?" and next, "Do you have any suggestions?"

This question shows respect for the person who will be affected by the decision. Susie is invited to share her expertise and judgment about appropriate consequences, and is encouraged to take direct responsibility for her actions.

If Susie makes a suggestion, the class is asked: "How many think this is a good suggestion?" If the majority of the class think the suggestion is acceptable, that suggestion is used to correct the problem and/or create logical consequences.

If Susie's suggestion is unacceptable, Jim is asked if he has a solution to recommend that would be helpful to Susie. Then other possibilities are solicited from class members. No more than five solutions are accepted for consideration. *Note:* Any solution or suggestion up for consideration by the class must meet the following requirements: It must be *related* to the incident, *reasonable, respectful,* and help students assume *responsibility* for their actions.

The suggestions are read and the class is asked to vote for the one they think would be most helpful to Susie. The solution that gets the most votes is the one selected.

Susie is given a choice about when the solution will be applied. For instance, if the solution was to have Susie skip a recess because of inappropriate playground behavior, the teacher will ask Susie if she wants to skip the next scheduled recess or the following recess. This is one way of guaranteeing that the child will not be ignored, discounted, or left out of any of the steps that will affect her.

The class is then asked if anyone has any tips for Susie so that she doesn't run into this problem again.

(A video training guide describing the Meder-Platt model for conducting classroom meetings may be purchased at a very nominal fee through the University Media Services, California State University, Sacramento, 6000 J Street, Sacramento, CA 95819.)

A Note About Alfred Adler (1870 – 1937)

Alfred Adler was a Viennese psychiatrist and one of this century's leading social scientists. Although he began his career as an ophthalmologist, he later turned to general practice and then to neurology. Adler viewed human beings as socially motivated and yet capable of dynamic, independent action. While he understood the influence of family and society on the development of personality and recognized the importance of understanding people within a social context, he believed that individuals create their own evaluations and choices about how to respond to life events. As early as 1900 he began addressing such crucial concepts and issues as equality, parent education, the influence of birth order, and contribution to the social welfare of all. He called his theory "individual psychology" to stress his focus on the unity of the individual.

Throughout his life he was particularly interested in educating parents and teachers in child-rearing practices. After serving as a medical officer in World War I, he established more than thirty child-guidance clinics in the Vienna schools. Teachers, parents, social workers, and physicians who attended these clinics learned how to understand and motivate children. Adler always emphasized the importance of developing children's confidence in their own strength. He believed that the child's greatest asset was the courage to face life's challenges. In 1935 the Nazis closed down all of Adler's clinics and he emigrated to the United States.

Today, Adlerian concepts are being used extensively in

education, community programs, business, counseling, and clinical practice. Alfred Adler's ideas and the ideas of those who followed in his footsteps will attain further importance as people continue to strive for greater democracy and fulfillment in living.

References

Adler, Alfred. *The Education of Children.* Chicago: Henry Regnery Company, 1970.

Ansbacher, H., and Ansbacher, R., eds. *The Individual Psychology of Alfred Adler.* New York: Harper & Row, 1956.

Bettner, B. L. "How to Produce a Friendly, Responsible, Capable, Cooperative, Resourceful Human Being." *Foster Care Journal,* January 1, 1984, 1–8.

Dreikurs, Rudolf, and Soltz, V. *Children: The Challenge.* New York: Hawthorn Books, 1964.

————; Corsini, R.; and Gould, S. *How to Stop Fighting with Your Kids.* New York: Ace Books, 1974.

Glenn, H. S., and Warner, J. *Developing Capable Young People.* Texas: Humansphere, 1982.

Lew, Amy. "Use and Misuse of Dreikursian Principles in Parent Education." *The Individual Psychologist,* 15, no. 2 (1978): 41–45.

Recommended Reading

General Parenting

Albert, Linda. *Coping with Kids and School: A Guide for Parents*. New York: E. P. Dutton, 1984.

———. *Linda Albert's Advice for Coping with Kids*. New York: E. P. Dutton, 1982.

Dinkmeyer, Don, and McKay, Gary. *Raising a Responsible Child*. New York: Simon and Schuster, 1973.

Dreikurs, Rudolf, and Soltz, V. *Children: The Challenge*. New York: Hawthorn Books, 1964.

Einstein, Elizabeth, and Albert, Linda. *Strengthening Your Stepfamily*. Circle Pines, Minn.: American Guidance Service, 1986.

Glenn, H. S., and Nelsen, J. *Raising Self-Reliant Children in a Self-Indulgent World*. Rocklin, Calif.: Prima Publishing & Communications, 1988.

Lott, L.: Intner, R.: and Krentz, M. *Family Work: Whose Job Is It?* Santa Rosa, Calif.: The Practical Press, 1983.

Main, Frank. *Perfect Parenting and Other Myths*. Minneapolis: CompCare Publishing, 1986.

Teens

Bayard, Jean, and Bayard, Robert T. *How to Deal with Your Acting-Up Teenager*. San Jose, Calif.: The Accord Press, 1981.

Walton, Francis X. *Winning Teenagers Over*. Columbia, S.C.: Adlerian Child Care Books, 1980.

Weinhaus, Evonne, and Friedman, Karen. *Stop Struggling with Your Child*. New York: HarperPerennial, 1991.

Weinhaus, Evonne, and Friedman, Karen. *Stop Struggling*

with Your Teen. New York: Viking Penguin, Inc., 1984, 1988.

Parent Education Programs

Dinkmeyer, Don, and McKay, Gary. *Systematic Training for Effective Parenting.* Circle Pines, Minn.: American Guidance Service, 1976. (Also available in Spanish.)

————. *Systematic Training for Effective Parenting of Teens.* Circle Pines, Minn.: American Guidance Service, 1978.

Popkin, Michael. *Active Parenting.* Atlanta: Active Parenting, 1983.

————. *Active Parenting of Teens.* Atlanta: Active Parenting, 1983.

Communication

Faber, Adele, and Mazlish, Elaine. *How to Talk So Kids Will Listen and Listen So Kids Will Talk.* New York: Avon Books, 1990.

Gordon, Thomas. *P.E.T.—Parent Effectiveness Training.* New York: Peter H. Wyden, 1970.

Encouragement/Self-Esteem

Dinkmeyer, Don, and Dreikurs, Rudolf. *Encouraging Children to Learn.* New York: Hawthorn Books, 1963.

Dinkmeyer, Don, and Losoncy, L. *The Encouragement Book: Becoming a Positive Person.* Englewood Cliffs, N.J.: Prentice-Hall, 1980.

Schools

Albert, Linda. *Cooperative Discipline.* Circle Pines, Minn.: American Guidance Service, 1989.

Brooks, Robert. *The Seeds of Self-Esteem* (video program). Circle Pines, Minn.: American Guidance Service, 1991.

————. *The Self-Esteem Teacher*. Circle Pines, Minn.: American Guidance Service, 1991.

Carlson, Jon, and Thorpe, Casey. *The Growing Teacher*. Englewood Cliffs, N.J.: Prentice-Hall, 1984.

Dinkmeyer, Don. *Developing Understanding of Self and Others*. Circle Pines, Minn.: American Guidance Service, 1970.

Dinkmeyer, Don; McKay, Gary; and Dinkmeyer, Don, Jr. *Systematic Training for Effective Teaching*. Circle Pines, Minn.: American Guidance Service, 1980.

Dreikurs, Rudolf. *Psychology in the Classroom* (Revised). New York: Harper & Row, 1957.

Dreikurs, Rudolf; Grunwald, B.; and Pepper, F. *Maintaining Sanity in the Classroom*. New York: Harper & Row, 1971.

Johnson, David W.; Johnson, Roger T.; and Holubec, Edythe Johnson. *Circles of Learning*. Edina, Minn.: Interaction Book Co., 1986.

Meder, F., and Platt, J. *Classroom Meetings* (video). Sacramento, Calif.: University Media Services, California State University.

Popkin, Michael. *Free the Horses: A Self-Esteem Adventure*. Atlanta: Active Parenting, 1991.

General Interest

Adler, Alfred. *What Life Should Mean to You*. Edited by Alan Porter. New York: Grosset and Dunlap, 1931.

Covey, Stephen R. *The 7 Habits of Highly Effective People*. New York: Simon and Schuster/Fireside, 1989.

Dreikurs, Rudolf. *The Challenge of Marriage*. New York: Hawthorn Books, 1964.

————. *Social Equality: The Challenge of Today*. Chicago: Alfred Adler Institute, 1971.

Kohn, Alfie. *No Contest*. Boston: Houghton Mifflin, 1986.